Praying *in the* Harvest

● ● ● ● ● ● ● ● ● ● ● ● ● ● ● ● ●

HOW TO PRAY FOR THE LOST

Praying *in the* Harvest

HOW TO PRAY FOR THE LOST

DON WALTON

GREEN KEY BOOKS
Holiday, Florida

PRAYING IN THE HARVEST
Don Walton
Published by Green Key Books

International Standard Book Number: 0-9705996-5-X

Cover Graphics: Ed Hendrix

All scripture quotations, unless otherwise indicated, are taken from
The King James Bible, public domain.

Scripture quotations marked (NIV) are taken from the Holy Bible, New International
Version®. NIV®. Copyright © 1973, 1978, 1984 by International Bible Society. Used
by permission of Zondervan. All rights reserved.

For information:
GREEN KEY BOOKS
2514 ALOHA PLACE
HOLIDAY, FLORIDA 34691
www.greenkeybooks.com

Library of Congress Catalog Card Number: 2001130798

Printed in the United States of America

TABLE OF CONTENTS

INTRODUCTION

Years ago, I asked my wife how she prayed for the lost. She answered, "I ask God to save them." "There must be more to it," I insisted. She replied, "It works for me." I may safely assume from your purchase of this book that you are already praying for the lost. Like my wife, you may feel that your present prayers for lost souls suffice. Far be it from me to suggest otherwise.

The intention of this book is not to provide a foolproof formula to be followed by all Christians in their prayers for lost souls. I know of no such formula. The only way I know to pray for the lost is under the leadership of the Holy Spirit. This book will make a poor substitute for God's Spirit in your prayer closet. Therefore, I implore you never to use it for that purpose, lest you rob your prayers of their potency.

What this book can do is point you to the multifaceted miracle of salvation. By doing so, it will drive you to your knees in adoration of Christ, Who snatched you as a brand from the fire with His loving nail-scarred hand, and also in intercession for the lost, whose dire and desperate plight is plainly presented on the pages of this volume.

After reading a rough draft of this manuscript, a friend suggested a change of title. He felt like the subject matter covered far more than prayer alone. Thus, he believed a broader title was warranted. Although I readily admit that this book is a serious study of our salvation in Christ, it retains its original title, thanks to the fact that my initial intent is still intact. My aim in writing this book is to aid you in your prayers for the lost. What better way to do so than by spreading out before you all that is involved in the salvation of a soul? By zeroing in on the particulars, we cannot help but make our prayers for the lost more effectual.

Don Walton
April 2001
Spring Hill, Florida

THE CONFLICT
by Don Walton

The prince of darkness and legion
go forth in this world to win
the invaluable prize of the conflict
the immortal souls of men.

Heaven aligns its forces.
The battle lines are drawn.
Eternities hang in the balance.
In fury the war rages on.

Humanities blind to the conflict,
though they the victor's spoil;
insensitive to the battle,
due to lives of earthly toil.

Where are God's gallant warriors,
who wax valiant in the fight,
who turn back the torrents of darkness
clad in the armor of light?

O Lord, chasten your children,
in haste wield the rod,
force to their knees your people
that they may rise and take hold of God.

Then, God's mighty princes
who are destined to prevail
will scale the citadels of evil
and snatch men from the clutches of hell.

Chapter 1

BIRTHED WITH A BURDEN

The most important thing in prayer is never our talking to God. Instead, it is God talking to us. Our best prayers are always initiated by God. They begin when we hear Him telling us how to pray. Until He does, we don't know who to pray for or what to pray about.

How many Christians today have a frustrated prayer life instead of a fruitful one simply because their prayers are self-initiated? Rather than permitting God to direct their prayer life, they decide for themselves who they want to pray for and what they want to pray about. Consequently, their prayers go unanswered and their objectives unattained. As James said, *"Ye ask, and receive not, because ye ask amiss, that ye may consume it upon your lusts"* (James 4:3).

The Apostle John writes: *"And this is the confidence that we have in him, that, if we ask anything according to his will, he heareth us: and if we know that he hear us, whatsoever we ask, we know that we have the petitions that we desired of him"* (I John 5:14–15). What a powerful promise! Here, we are promised the possibility of praying a prayer that can't miss. All that is required of us is to pray according to God's will and not ours.

If you and I want to have a powerful prayer life, we must stop viewing prayer as an attempt on our part to win God over to our side. Instead, we must start seeing prayer as a time for us to go over to God's side. Prayer is not us trying to talk God into doing what we want. Prayer is us asking God to do what He wants. When we start praying for God's will to be done, rather than our own, we'll be praying prayers that can't miss.

WORLD RESPONSIBILITY SYNDROME

When it comes to praying for the lost some Christians have "WORLD RESPONSIBILITY SYNDROME." They feel as though it is their responsibility to pray for the salvation of every lost person in the world. They may attempt to meet this responsibility by praying simple Tiny-Tim-like prayers: "God save everyone." However, if they take this responsibility more seriously they're in for a stressed-out prayer life. After all, what Christian can single-handedly bear the burden of a lost and dying world in his personal prayer closet or pray his way through a prayer list as long as our world's lost population?

A few years ago, I read a magazine article about a prominent preacher's bout with burnout. According to him, one of the major contributors to his burnout was his prayer list, which had become so long and burdensome that he dreaded going into his prayer closet. Prayer had ceased being a delight and had become a drudgery.

The Bible teaches us that prayer should release us from our anxieties *(Philippians 4:6–7)*. It should never become one of the reasons for them. Still, just like the prominent preacher in the aforementioned magazine article, prayer has become a source of stress to too many Christians. Feeling duty bound to pray for too many people, they find themselves stumbling beneath the load of their overloaded prayer life.

INTERCEDE AS GOD LEADS

If it is not our responsibility to pray for every lost soul in the world, then what is our responsibility? Our responsibility is to pray for every lost soul for whom God burdens us to pray. Furthermore, we can rest assured that the prayers we pray under God-given burdens will always prove to be of great avail; otherwise, God would not have burdened us to pray.

The great preacher, Charles Haddon Spurgeon, was once confronted by a young woman in great distress over the burden she bore for her lost mother. Her burden for her mother's soul was so great that it drove her to her knees in prayer both day and night. She feared that being so burdened in prayer for her mom may have pointed to the improbability of her mother's salvation.

After hearing of her God-given burden for her mother's soul, Spurgeon asked the young woman about the spiritual condition of her father. The young woman explained to the great preacher that her father, just like her mother, was lost and without Christ. However, she wasn't burdened to pray for her father's soul like she was her mother's. In light of this, Spurgeon assured the young woman that she should be far more concerned about the improbability of her father's salvation than the improbability of her mother's.

Prayer for the lost is birthed with a burden. It begins when God burdens us to pray for some lost soul. When we're burdened by God to pray for the lost, we can be assured that our prayers will not go unheard or unheeded. They will prove to be of great avail. If they would not, God would not have burdened us to pray!

PRAYER

"Speak, Lord, for your servant listens. Direct my prayers according to your will, not my own. Burden my heart for those lost souls you want me to pray for. And may the prayers I pray for them, birthed by the burdens you give to me, prove to be of great avail! Amen."

Chapter 2

The Prayer Of Faith

I s healing in the atonement? This is one of the most explosive questions in Christendom today, yet the Scripture is quite clear on the subject. According to the ancient prophet Isaiah, Jesus Christ *"took our infirmities, and bore our sicknesses…and with his stripes we are healed" (Isaiah 53:4–5)*. "Yes, but this is talking about spiritual healing, not physical healing," you protest. That's not what Matthew 8:14–17 teaches us. Matthew says that Jesus healed the physically afflicted so *"that it might be fulfilled which was spoken by Esaias [Isaiah] the prophet, saying, Himself took our infirmities, and bore our sicknesses."*

Contrary to the opinion of many, Isaiah is talking about physical healing. Are we to conclude then that Christians should never be sick or that they should always be healed of every illness they contract? Not at all. We all know that Christians are no more immune to sickness than unbelievers. Neither are all Christians healed of all their diseases. Nevertheless, there is one thing of which we can be certain. If it were not for Christ's atoning death, there would be no divine healing at all.

God is sovereign. It is up to Him who is healed and who is not. Those who are healed need to thank Christ for it because, without His death on the cross, their healing would have never occurred.

Along with taking *"our infirmities"* and bearing *"our sick-nesses,"* Isaiah also says that Jesus *"was wounded for our trans-gressions...bruised for our iniquities...and the Lord hath laid on him the iniquity of us all"* (Isaiah 53:5–6). According to the Apostle John, Christ did not die for our sins only *"but also for the sins of the whole world"* (I John 2:2). Since Jesus died for every sin of everybody, does this mean that everybody is forgiven and saved from sin? Absolutely not! It only means that without Christ's atoning death no one would ever be forgiven or saved.

THE DOCTRINE OF ELECTION

God alone decides who will be saved. He does not, however, decide who will be condemned. That decision has already been made. The Bible states, *"For God sent not his Son into the world to con-demn the world; but that the world through him might be saved. He that believeth on him is not condemned: but he that believeth not is condemned already, because he hath not believed in the name of the only begotten Son of God"* (John 3:17–18). The entire world, includ-ing you and me, is condemned already. We have already made this decision for ourselves. As Isaiah says, *"All we like sheep have gone astray; we have turned everyone to his own way."*

Although our condemnation has been decided by us, our sal-vation is decided by God alone. The Bible says that God decided our salvation before He laid *"the foundation of the world"* (Ephesians 1:4). Before any of us were born, God had already decided whom He would call as His own and whom He would set apart for Himself *(Romans 9:10–13; Jeremiah 1:5)*.

Many today take exception with this clear teaching in Scripture. They insist that our salvation is determined by our decision for Christ. Yet, this is not what Jesus taught. In John 15:16, Jesus said, *"Ye have not chosen me, but I have chosen you."* Our choice of Christ is merely a consequence of Christ's prior choice of us.

Does this mean that God chooses to condemn some and save others? Of course not! God doesn't choose to condemn anyone. The Bible says that God is *"not willing that any should perish, but that all should come to repentance" (2 Peter 3:9)*. God doesn't want anyone to be condemned. Then why are we condemned? We are condemned because of our choice not God's. We choose sin over Christ for ourselves. It is this decision of ours that condemns us.

The only choice God makes is the one concerning our salvation not our condemnation. God doesn't choose for any of us to be condemned. We make that decision for ourselves. God only chooses those who will be saved. While no one will ever be condemned because of God's choice, none of us can ever be saved without it.

THE NEED TO INTERCEDE

Because of the doctrine of election, many have erroneously concluded that there is no reason to pray for the lost. After all, what good does it do to pray for the salvation of those whom God has not chosen? And why bother praying for God's elect? They will be saved with or without our prayers. Although it is true that our prayers will never result in the salvation of those whom God has not chosen, it is untrue that our prayers for God's elect are unnecessary.

It is not God's choice or election of men that saves them. True, they cannot be saved without it, but it is not what saves them.

According to the Apostle Paul, God is *"pleased by the foolishness of preaching to save them that believe" (1 Corinthians 1:21)*. The only way God's elect can be saved is if the gospel is preached to them and they believe. Thus, the doctrine of election does not render our preaching of the gospel and praying for the lost unnecessary. Instead, it makes them both essential. Although the elect will be saved, for God will not not fail to fulfill His eternal purpose in election, God's plan for the salvation of the elect is dependent upon our faithfulness in preaching the gospel and praying for the lost.

THE PRAYER OF FAITH

In James 5:15, we are told that *"the prayer of faith shall save the sick, and the Lord shall raise him up."* Where does faith come from? According to Romans 10:17, *"Faith cometh by hearing, and hearing by the word of God."* Faith comes from hearing God for ourselves. When God tells us He has chosen to heal someone, faith is born in our heart. We can then pray the prayer of faith over the one who is sick. Consequently, God will heal him and raise him up. All of this is made possible by Christ's atoning death on the cross where He took *"our infirmities"* and bore *"our sicknesses."*

Likewise, when we hear God tell us someone is chosen by Him for salvation, faith is born in our heart. We can then pray the prayer of faith for that lost soul. Consequently, God will save that person and raise him up from his death in trespasses and sins. All of this, too, is made possible by Christ's atoning death on the cross where He *"was wounded for our transgressions"* and *"bruised for our iniquities."*

Notice, whether it is healing or salvation, it is up to a sovereign God to choose the recipients, yet neither would be available to those whom God chooses were it not for what Christ did for us all on the cross. When God speaks to us concerning His choice of someone, for healing or salvation, faith is immediately born in our heart. We know what God is going to do for such individuals. If they are sick, we know God is going to heal them. If they are lost, we know God is going to save them. Therefore, we can pray the prayer of faith over them so that God can work His miracle for them.

LABORERS TOGETHER WITH GOD

In 1 Corinthians 3:9, the Apostle Paul writes, *"For we are labourers together with God."* By saving those He chooses through our preaching and praying, God permits us to partner with Him in carrying out His purposes in this world. What greater thrill can any of us ever experience than to be laboring together with a sovereign God in His saving of men's immortal souls?

PRAYER

"I praise you, O sovereign God. I thank you for your Son Jesus Christ. I acknowledge this day that the gift of salvation you have elected to give me from your gracious hand is made possible by the atoning death of your beloved Son. I ask you now to speak to my heart concerning your elect so that I may partner with you in their salvation by praying for them the prayer of faith! Amen."

Don Walton

Chapter 3

THE BLOOD OF JESUS

U pon what legal ground do we justify our prayers for the salvation of men's souls? In praying for the lost, it is imperative that we understand the legal ground that we kneel upon because this understanding enables us to rise up and take hold of God in this most solemn matter *(Isaiah 64:7)*.

THE CREATION OF MAN

The Psalmist writes: *"The earth is the Lord's, and the fullness thereof; the world, and they that dwell therein" (Psalm 24:1)*. In Psalm 100:3, God's proprietorship over us is attributed to His creation of us. Here, we read, *"Know ye that the Lord he is God, it is he that hath made us, and not we ourselves; we are his people, and the sheep of his pasture."* Since God created us, we all belong to Him. All souls belong to God as He Himself boldly declares in Ezekiel 18:4: *"Behold, all souls are mine."*

It is God's ownership of all souls that justifies our prayers for their salvation, yet it is also on this precise point—the ownership of all souls by their Creator—that some will raise an objection. They will argue that only saved souls belong to God and that all lost souls belong to the devil.

Speaking to some lost souls in John 8:44, Jesus said, *"Ye are of your father the devil, and the lusts of your father ye will do."* It is true as our Lord insinuates in this verse that the devil claims all lost souls for himself. However, the Bible teaches that he does so illegally.

THE FALL OF MAN

In Luke 4:5–8, the devil tempts Christ to worship him by offering our Lord the kingdoms of this world. In verse 6, the devil assures Christ that he can give Him the kingdoms of the world because they were *"delivered"* to him. The Greek word translated "delivered" means "betrayed." Interestingly, our Lord neither disputes Satan's seemingly outlandish claim to the world nor the fact that the world has been betrayed into Satan's hands.

When was this world betrayed into the hands of Satan? The answer to this question is found in the third chapter of Genesis. In the first two chapters of Genesis, we read about God's creating man and giving him dominion over all the earth. Then, in the third chapter—the darkest chapter in all of the Bible—we read about man's betrayal of God and handing over to Satan this world's dominion.

Ever since man betrayed the world into Satan's hands, Satan has exercised dominion over the world. Satan may have acquired his dominion over the world through treachery, but he acquired it nonetheless. This is why Jesus called the devil *"the prince of this world" (John 12:31, 14:30)*. It is why the Apostle Paul called him *"the god of this world" (2 Corinthians 4:4)*. And it is why the Apostle

John taught that *"the whole world is under the control of the evil one"* (*I John 5:19,* NIV).

THE REDEMPTION OF MAN

In spite of Satan's treachery, God has prevailed in this legal battle for the souls of men. The central message of the Bible is that God sent His Son into the world to redeem mankind. To redeem something means to buy it back. Everything lost to Satan through man's treason in the garden has been bought back for God by the shed blood of Jesus Christ.

In John 12:31, Jesus said, *"Now is the judgment of this world; now shall the prince of this world be cast out."* Jesus made this statement in the shadow of the cross. He knew His impending death would prove to be the devil's undoing. By shedding His blood on the cross, Christ stripped Satan of all legal claims to any earthly possessions. It is the shed blood of Jesus Christ that cast out *"the prince of this world."*

Suppose you returned from vacation and discovered a squatter living in your home. You insist to the trespasser that he vacate the premises, but he refuses to leave. How can you cast out this trespasser? You can do so by producing the title to your home, proving your ownership of it. With the title, you have a legal claim to your house and the legal right to evict the intruder.

In the fifth chapter of Revelation, the Apostle John sees *"in the right hand of him that sat on the throne a book written within and on the backside, sealed with seven seals."* I believe that this book in God's right hand is the title deed to the earth. A search is made for someone *"worthy to open the book, and loose the seals thereof."* Unfortunately, *"no man in heaven, nor in earth, was able to open the book, neither to look thereon."* Consequently, John began to weep. While he wept, one of the twenty-four elders, which sit around the throne of God, spoke to him. The elder told John to *"weep not"* because *"the Lion of the tribe of Judah, the Root of David, hath prevailed to open the book, and to loose the seven seals thereof."* When John looked up he saw *"in the midst of the throne and of the four beasts and in the midst of the elders...a Lamb as it had been slain."* John watched as the Lamb went to the throne of God and took the book out of God's right hand. When the Lamb took the book from the hand of God, all of Heaven erupted in *"a new song, saying, 'Thou art worthy to take the book, and to open the seals thereof: for thou wast slain, and hast redeemed us to God by thy blood out of every kindred, and tongue, and people, and nation; and hast made us unto our God kings and priests: and we shall reign on the earth.'"*

Jesus Christ holds the title deed to the earth. It is His shed blood that has bought back everything for God that man betrayed into the hands of Satan. Therefore, God has a legal claim to the earth and all its inhabitants. He also has the legal right to evict *"the prince of this world"* wherever he is found trespassing.

THE LEGAL GROUND WE KNEEL UPON

The legal ground we kneel upon when praying for the lost is at the foot of the cross. From this blood-stained soil, we can lawfully cry out to Heaven for the salvation of men's souls. Nothing is more important in our prayers for the lost than our pleading for the blood of Jesus Christ **over** them.

Jesus shed His blood for all men *(John 1:29, 3:17; 2 Corinthians 5:15; Hebrews 2:9; 1 John 2:2)* By doing so, He redeemed us all.[1] According to the Apostle Peter, Jesus has even bought back for God those who deny Him *(2 Peter 2:1)*. Now, this doesn't mean that all men are saved, but only that all men are God's. In order to be saved, *"the redeemed of the Lord say so" (Psalm 107:2)*. As the Apostle Paul puts it in Romans 10:9–10, *"That if thou shalt confess with thy mouth the Lord Jesus, and shalt believe in thine heart that God hath raised him from the dead, thou shalt be saved. For with the heart man believeth unto righteousness; and with the mouth confession is made unto salvation."*

The blood of Jesus Christ does not make all men the children of God. It makes them the property of God. Only those who receive Jesus Christ by faith become God's children *(John 1:12)*. The rest of mankind, though not in God's family, are in His possession; they are legally His. Hence, we can justly pray for the salvation of their souls and Satan's eviction from their lives.

PRAYER

"I praise you, O God, the Creator, Redeemer, and Owner of our souls. I kneel this day upon the blood-stained soil of Calvary to plead the blood of Jesus over lost souls for whom you have burdened me. I ask that Satan, the trespasser, be evicted from the lives of the redeemed. I pray that the redeemed of the Lord will say so by confessing the Lord Jesus Christ. I also ask that those already in your possession will now come into your family by receiving from your Son the power to become your children! Amen."

Don Walton

Chapter 4
THE LORD OF THE HARVEST

In Matthew 9:38 and Luke 10:2, Jesus instructs us to pray to *"the Lord of the harvest, that he will send forth labourers into his harvest."* Who is the Lord of the harvest? Obviously, God is. God alone gives the harvest. He may use us to plant or water, but He alone *"giveth the increase" (1 Corinthians 3:5–7)*.

When will today's church learn that harvesting souls is not a matter of better marketing, contemporary services, and church programs? It requires a miracle of God! In Acts 2:47, we read how *"the Lord added to the church daily such as should be saved."* Only the Lord can add to His church. We may add to ours by building a family life center, recruiting a church softball team, or incorporating a praise band into our Sunday morning repertoire. Still, only God can save a soul *(Isaiah 43:11)*.

A famous evangelist was once asked by a staggering drunk if he remembered him. When the evangelist responded, "No," the drunk said, "You saved me in one of your meetings." To this the evangelist replied, "You look like a job I would do." Unfortunately, many people in today's church look like a job we have done. They don't resemble a work of God at all. They look more like a convert of ours than they do a convert of Christ's.

Not only is the Lord of the harvest the only One who can give the harvest, He is also the only One who can send laborers into His harvest. In today's church, we often try to draft an army for God. We attempt to recruit laborers for the fields by shaming the saints or by threatening them with guilt if they refuse to go. Today's pastors often resort to warning congregations that the blood of lost souls will be on their hands throughout eternity if they don't share their faith with everyone who crosses their path.

In spite of all our scary rhetoric and strong-armed recruiting, less than 5% of those who profess to know Christ have ever introduced Him to anyone else. Maybe, in light of this, it's time we burn our draft cards. Instead of spending so much time attempting to recruit laborers for the fields, we should spend more time praying to *"the Lord of the harvest, that he will send forth labourers into his harvest"* because only He can grant the harvest and send out the laborers to gather it in.

WHITE FIELDS

As the Lord's field hands, we are to go only where He sends us. Too many Christians take it upon themselves to force feed the Bread of Life to everyone they meet. They do not hesitate to shove the gospel down some stranger's throat in the most inappropriate place and at the most inopportune time. Such confrontations rarely, if ever, result in real conversions. They do run the risk, however, of spiritually choking to death some poor unsuspecting sinner.

The Lord of the harvest will only send us to pick ripe fruit. Those He sends us to will be ready to harvest or at least be receptive to the planting or watering of the gospel seed. On the other hand, if we attempt on our own initiative to pick unripe fruit, we will certainly end up frustrated, never fruitful. We may even bruise the fruit so that it will never ripen for the harvest.

In the fourth chapter of John's Gospel, Jesus, much to the disgust of His disciples, decided to travel through Samaria on His way to Galilee. The reason for this change in route was a divine appointment Jesus had with a woman at a well in Sychar. This woman was thirsty for living water. Her soul's thirst was forever satisfied when she met the Savior. Afterward, she ran throughout her village telling all the men, *"Come, see a man, which told me all things that ever I did: is not this the Christ?" (John 4.29)*

As a result of the woman's testimony, the men of the village came out to the well to meet Jesus for themselves. With their white robes blowing in the wind, Jesus pointed to the approaching Samaritans and said to His disciples, *"Say not ye, 'There are yet four months, and then cometh harvest?' behold, I say unto you, Lift up your eyes, and look on the fields; for they are white already to harvest."* Jesus led His disciples to Sychar of Samaria because there were white fields to be harvested, and consequently, *"many of the Samaritans of that city believed on him."*

We can rest assured that wherever and whenever Christ leads us to witness there is a harvest waiting to be gathered. Granted, Christ may not use our witness to reap the harvest. He may use us to merely plant or water the seed of the gospel in the good soil of a receptive heart. Still, in Christ's time and in His way, someone will be sent by Him to reap where we have labored. This is exactly what Jesus spoke about in Samaria when He said to His disciples:

And he that reapeth receiveth wages, and gathereth fruit unto life eternal: that both he that soweth and he that reapeth may rejoice together. And herein is that saying true, One soweth, and another reapeth. I sent you to reap that whereon ye bestowed no labour: other men laboured, and ye are entered into their labours (John 4:36–38).

THE PRAYER OF DISPATCH

One of the most important prayers we can ever pray for lost souls is that the Lord of the harvest will dispatch a laborer to gather them into His garner. This laborer may be us. Therefore, we must be very sensitive to any leading and opportunity that the Lord gives us to share our faith. This sensitivity to the Lord in sharing our faith should not be confined to those specific lost souls for whom we are burdened. For all we know, the Lord of the harvest may dispatch us at any time in any place to gather some fruit into eternal life as a consequence of others' prayers on behalf of lost souls for whom they are burdened.

Whether it is we or our fellow laborers who are sent, we need to pray that the Lord of the harvest will dispatch laborers to witness to those lost souls for whom we are burdened. The Bible promises us that the lost we are burdened for *"shall be saved"* if they *"call upon the name of the Lord" (Romans 10:13),* and yet the Apostle Paul asked, *"How then shall they call on him in whom they have not believed? and how shall they believe in him of whom they have not heard? and how shall they hear without a preacher? And how shall they preach except they be sent?" (Romans 10:14–15).*

Contrary to popular opinion, I don't believe that the Apostle Paul is insinuating in this passage that the salvation of lost souls is contingent upon the church sending out missionaries through our giving. Instead, I believe Paul is teaching that the salvation of lost souls is contingent upon the Lord of the harvest sending forth laborers into His harvest through our prayers. This in no way should be miscued to undermine the importance of missions. Just as God sends us into His fields with the gospel, He also uses us to send others into the far distant fields of our world. Still, in the end, it is God that does the sending.

Only the Lord of the harvest can send the right laborer into the right field at the right time to gather fruit into His garner. Only the Lord of the harvest knows when the heart of a sinner is ripe and ready to be picked for the Kingdom of God. And only the Lord of the harvest can break up the fallow ground of a sinful heart preparing it for the planting and watering of the seed of the gospel. Thus, if we hope to see our lost friends and loved ones gathered by God's grace into His garner, we must pray to the Lord of the harvest on their behalf.

PRAYER

"I praise you, O God, for apart from you there is no Savior. I pray to you, Lord of the harvest, that you will send forth laborers into your harvest, for the harvest is great, but the laborers are few. Please dispatch me or a fellow laborer to the lost souls for whom I am burdened so that they may be gathered into your garner. And daily lift up my eyes to see the fields that are white to harvest so that I may be used by you to gather fruit unto eternal life. Amen."

Don Walton

Chapter 5
PRAYING FOR
THOSE IN AUTHORITY

J. Vernon McGee, the famous radio Bible teacher, was once asked why he did not run for political office. He answered, "God did not call me to clean up the pond, but only to fish in it." I'm afraid most Christians today, unlike the late Dr. McGee, are more committed to politics than they are to preaching.

Christians need to learn that our world will never be changed through the political process. Our world will never change until men change. Although politics may change public policy, it is powerless to change people. Only the Gospel of Jesus Christ has the power to transform men. This means that the church alone, as the sole steward of the Gospel of Jesus Christ, has the power to change the world.

However, this awesome power, solely possessed by the church, is only wielded by us when we are preaching the gospel. When we exchange preaching for political activism, the church becomes powerless to effect change in the world. Is there any wonder then that the devil is working so diligently today to deceive the church into cleaning up the pond as an alternative to fishing in it?

Rendering To Caesar

In Luke 20:25, Jesus said, *"Render therefore unto Caesar the things which be Caesar's, and unto God the things which be God's."* As Christians, we hold a dual citizenship. First and foremost, we are citizens of Heaven. Second, we are citizens of the state. As a result of our dual citizenship, we have responsibilities to both God and Caesar, so it is important that we render to both their dues.

One of the things owed to Caesar is our prayers. In 1 Timothy 2:1–4, the Apostle Paul writes: *"I exhort therefore, that, first of all, supplications, prayers, intercessions, and giving of thanks, be made for all men; For kings, and for all that are in authority; that we may lead a quiet and peaceable life in all godliness and honesty. For this is good and acceptable in the sight of God our Saviour; Who will have all men to be saved, and to come unto the knowledge of the truth."*

In exhorting us to pray *"for all men"* Paul singles out *"kings and all that are in authority."* Why? Is God more concerned with the powerful than the populace? No, unlike our world, God is no respecter of persons *(Acts 10:34)*. In His eyes, there is no difference between potentates and peasants.

The reason we are exhorted to pray especially for political leaders is because they hold such sway over the quality of life in our society. It is not because they have some special favor with God. Rather, it is because they have such influence over our way of life.

Proverbs 21:1 teaches us: *"The king's heart is in the hand of the Lord, as the rivers of water: he turneth it whithersoever he will."* If we clasp our hands in prayer for political leaders, God, who holds their hearts in His hand, can sway them to keep our society *"quiet and peaceable.*" In such a society, Christians can practice their faith, publicly worship their Lord, and propagate their land with the gospel. According to Paul, *"this is good and acceptable in the sight of God our Saviour; Who will have all men to be saved, and to come unto the knowledge of the truth."*

Notice, the reason *"God our Saviour"* wants a *"quiet and peaceable"* society is so that men will *"be saved and come unto the knowledge of the truth."* Where is it easier for sinners to be saved and learn of Christ—in a Muslim land where Christians are arrested for witnessing to others, in a Communist land where the church is prohibited from preaching the gospel, or in a free society where the church is permitted to practice and proclaim its faith? Obviously, the easiest place for sinners to be saved is in a free society. This is why God wants us praying especially for our political leaders.

God is not concerned with politics, although politicians often claim He is on their side. God's concern is with the preaching of the Gospel of Jesus Christ. God cares for our political leaders. He cares just as much, however, for their constituency. God wants all men from the White House to your house to have the opportunity to hear the gospel and be saved. Thus, He instructs us to pray *"for all men"* but especially *"for kings, and all that are in authority"* so that we will have a *"quiet and peaceable"* society in which everyone will have an opportunity to hear the gospel and *"come to the knowledge of the truth."*

Reinterpreting The Constitution

Praying for our leaders so that our society will remain open to the public proclamation of the gospel may seem unnecessary to many Christians in America. They take it for granted that our constitution guarantees us the right to publicly practice and proclaim our faith. Why then should we bother praying to our Heavenly Father for something our founding fathers have already guaranteed us?

In case you haven't noticed, strange things are currently abreast in America—things which our founding fathers would have never believed. Our constitution is being reinterpreted by today's courts and political leaders to say things that our founding fathers never imagined, much less intended. For instance, the separation of church and state provided by the First Amendment of our constitution was intended by our founding fathers to prohibit government from interfering with the free exercise of religion. Today, however, the First Amendment has been reinterpreted to prohibit people with religious beliefs from being involved in government. According to the reinterpreters of our constitution, the Christian faith should be expelled from the public square and exiled to our private lives. Public displays of our faith, such as prayer in the public schools, are now being called unconstitutional.

In view of the reinterpretation of our constitution by today's courts and political leaders, it is no longer far-fetched to foresee a day in America when every public expression of our Christian faith will be deemed unconstitutional. Could the day be fast approaching when even the church's public proclamation of the gospel will be outlawed in America? Although such a thing was once unimaginable in these United States, it is now certainly plausible and possibly looming.

In the past, we may have considered praying for those in authority to be of minor importance. We did so because we took for granted our right to publicly practice and proclaim our Christian faith. We are now learning the fallacy of our past naiveté. Far from being of minor importance, praying for our society to remain free and open to the public proclamation of the gospel is of major concern. Our prayers for those in authority are some of the most crucial we can pray for the lost in America because, if we fail to pray for the leaders of our nation, we may soon lose the freedom to preach to the lost of our land.

PRAYER

"I praise you, God our Savior, for you hold the hearts of kings in your hand. I pray that you will keep our society free, quiet, and peaceable by turning the hearts of all in authority whithersoever you will. Use those in authority to keep the gospel from being silenced in our land so that all men will have an opportunity to come to the knowledge of the truth and be saved. Amen."

Don Walton

Chapter 6
GOD'S SECRET SERVICE

Before the four winds of the earth are unleashed in Revelation chapter seven, angels are dispatched to seal 144,000 Jews. Twelve thousand are sealed from each of the twelve tribes of Israel. Many believe that these Jews will propagate the world with the gospel message during the Tribulation Period. They point to the great multitude in Revelation chapter seven as proof of the proficiency of these Jewish evangelists. This *"great multitude, which no man could number, of all nations, and kindreds, and people, and tongues"* is supposedly comprised of the converts of the 144,000. If this is so, the greatest revival of all time will occur on the earth after Christ has raptured His church, God has removed His Spirit, and the devil is given free reign. Though this belief is popular with many, it is preposterous to me!

There is no evidence in all of Scripture to support such a great revival during the Tribulation. Quite to the contrary, Scripture is replete with contradictions of such a notion. For instance, in Revelation 13:3–4, John sees *"all the world"* worshipping and wondering *"after the beast"* during the Tribulation Period. He also records in Revelation 11:10 how that *"they that dwell upon the earth shall rejoice"* when the Antichrist kills God's two witnesses. While the dead bodies of God's witnesses lay in the street of Jerusalem,

29

the world will *"make merry, and shall send gifts one to another."* This doesn't sound like a time of great revival to me. It sounds more like Christmas time for the devil.

In 2 Thessalonians 2:7–12, the Apostle Paul teaches that God will send a *"strong delusion"* into the world following the rapture of Christ's church. According to Paul, God does this so that those who neither loved nor believed the truth will *"believe a lie"* and *"be damned."* So much for the multitude which turned its nose up at Christ before the rapture to afterward turn to Him in a great revival.

In Luke 18:8, Christ asked the question, *"When the Son of man cometh, shall he find faith on the earth?"* Far from finding revival at His return, Christ questions whether He will find any faith at all when He returns. In light of this question of our Lord, a great revival during the Tribulation appears totally out of the question.

The great multitude of Revelation chapter seven is not comprised of converts won in a great revival during the Tribulation by the 144,000. Instead, this great multitude is the raptured church of the Lord Jesus Christ. Some will protest that this cannot possibly be true since the multitude is said to have *"come out of great tribulation."* Believing that the church is raptured before the Tribulation, most premillennialists find any association of this multitude with the church completely untenable. But how do my fellow-premillennialists' reconcile their insistence upon a pretribulation rapture with the teaching of the Apostle Paul in 2 Thessalonians 2:1–12?

The Thessalonians had been deceived into believing that the rapture had already taken place. For this reason, Paul wrote Second Thessalonians to assure the church in Thessalonica that such was not the case. According to Paul, two things have to take place before the rapture occurs. First, there must be a *"falling away."* The Greek word Paul uses here for "falling away" means "apostasy." Before the rapture occurs, there will be a great apostasy in the church. Second, the rapture will not occur until the *"man of sin is revealed, the son of perdition."*

What is it that reveals the Antichrist or, as Paul calls him, *"the man of sin"* or *"the son of perdition"*? According to Jesus, it is *"the abomination of desolation, spoken of by Daniel the prophet"* *(Matthew 24:15–22)*. Daniel places the abomination of desolation in the middle of the Tribulation Period *(Daniel 9:27)*. The Great Tribulation begins with this abominable act of the Antichrist and culminates in the Second Coming of Jesus Christ.

If the rapture does not occur until the Antichrist is revealed by the abomination of desolation, the rapture will, then, take place during the Great Tribulation. Thus, there is no contradiction in identifying the great multitude of Revelation chapter seven as the raptured church of Christ despite the fact that this multitude *"comes out of great tribulation."*

SAFETY SEALED

The 144,000 of Revelation chapter seven are not sealed to preach the gospel during the Tribulation. They are sealed for their protection during the Tribulation. According to the Bible, only a remnant of the Jewish people will survive the Tribulation. This remnant, represented by the 144,000 of Revelation chapter seven, will turn to Christ when He returns.

All of this is prophesied by the ancient prophet Zechariah in the final three chapters of his prophecy (chapters 12–14). According to Zechariah, the surviving Jewish remnant will ask Christ at His return, *"What are these wounds in thine hands?"* When Christ responds, *"Those with which I was wounded in the house of my friends,"* the surviving remnant will at long last realize that Christ is the Jewish Messiah. God will then *"pour upon the house of David, and upon the inhabitants of Jerusalem, the spirit of grace and of supplications: and they shall look upon* [Christ] *whom they have pierced, and they shall mourn for him, as one mourneth for his only son, and shall be in bitterness for him, as one that is in bitterness for his firstborn."*

Zechariah compares the mourning of the Jewish remnant at Christ's return to *"the mourning of Hadadrimmon in the valley of Megiddon."* It was at Hadad Rimmon, a village in the valley of the plain of Megiddo, that Judah's godly king Josiah was slain by Egypt's Pharaoh Neco. Josiah represented the last hope for the fading kingdom of Judah. His death, therefore, was an occasion of unprecedented mourning throughout the land. How much more shall the mourning of Israel be upon realizing that the lowly Nazarene it crucified long ago was none other than its promised Messiah?

As the surviving Jewish remnant mourns over the Christ they crucified, God will *"remove the iniquity of* [their] *land in one day"* *(Zechariah 3:9)*. On that day, the day of Christ's return, *"all Israel shall be saved"* *(Romans 11:26–27)*. Don't forget, however, that if the Jewish remnant had not been sealed by the angels they would have never survived the Tribulation to be saved on the day of Christ's return.

HEAVEN'S SECRET SERVICE

Protecting God's elect until the day of salvation appears to be a part of the ministry of angels. In Hebrews 1:14, we are taught that angels are *"ministering spirits, sent forth to minister for them who shall be heirs of salvation."* Notice the future tense employed in this verse: *"who shall be heirs of salvation."* Angels minister to those who shall be saved but who have not yet come to Christ. How do they minister to these future *"heirs of salvation"*? I believe in the same way that they minister to the 144,000 of Revelation chapter seven. They safeguard God's elect so that the elect will survive until the day of their salvation.

All of us have heard fellow believers testify about the miracle of their survival while they were lost and living in sin. The fact that they were not killed during those days of riotous living is astonishing to them. Perhaps, they miraculously survived a horrible automobile accident or even more miraculously were never in one despite the fact that they often drove under the influence of drugs or alcohol. Although they are grateful to have been spared from the fate of a premature grave, many of our fellow believers still grieve for former accomplices in sin who were not so fortunate.

Does all of this not point to the possibility of angelic intervention in the lives of the saints while they were still sinners? We all know that angels intervene in the lives of God's saints following their salvation. Scripture contains so many post-salvation instances of angelic intervention on behalf of God's servants that no one can deny this possibility. God even promises to *"give his angels charge over"* everyone who makes Him their *"refuge"* so that His angels can *"keep thee in all thy ways"* and *"bear thee up in their hands, lest thou dash thy foot against a stone" (Psalm 91:9–12)*. But what about pre-salvation instances of angelic intervention in the lives of God's saints? Does God really dispatch angels to safeguard those *"who shall be heirs of salvation"* so that they will survive until the day of their salvation? Again, Hebrews 1:14 emphatically answers this question in the affirmative: *"Are they not all ministering spirits, sent forth to minister for them who shall be heirs of salvation?"*

Since man fell with the aid of a fallen angel, it is only fitting that he should be regenerated with the aid of unfallen ones. Assisting men in their regeneration by safeguarding them until the day of their salvation makes the heavenly host God's secret service. It also helps us to understand why there is such rejoicing *"in the presence of the angels of God over one sinner that repenteth" (Luke 15:10)*. Every time a sinner repents, Heaven's secret service has succeeded in safeguarding another soul into the fold of the Good Shepherd.

Praying For Those On Sin's Death Row

In Acts 12:1–12, Herod kills the Apostle James and imprisons the Apostle Peter. The night before Peter's execution God dispatches an angel who miraculously delivers Peter from prison. All of this takes place in response to the prayers of the church for Peter's protection.

The lost of our world are imprisoned. They are imprisoned on sin's death row. The threat of execution continually hangs over their heads. Any day could be execution day. For this reason, we should pray to God for the protection of those lost souls for whom we are burdened. In response to our prayers, God will dispatch His angels to miraculously deliver our lost friends and family from sin's gallows so that they can safely come to God's Son.

PRAYER

"I praise you, O Lord, for you are as superior to the angels as your name is to theirs. I pray that you will send forth your angels to minister for them who shall be heirs of salvation. May the lost for whom I am burdened be sealed and safeguarded by your angels until the day of their salvation. Afterward, give your angels continuing charge over them, lest they dash their foot against a stone. Amen."

Don Walton

Chapter 7
IT TAKES A MIRACLE

Evangelicals have long condemned the false doctrine of *baptismal regeneration*. To suggest that the performance of a church ritual in our infancy assures us of salvation is absurd—just as absurd as believing that anyone who has been baptized is a shoo-in for Heaven. While we justly condemn such heretical teaching, we need to take care that we do not become guilty of something akin to it. Many evangelicals today, though continuing the good fight against *baptismal regeneration*, are falling prey to what may be called *decisional regeneration*.

DECISIONAL REGENERATION

What is *decisional regeneration*? It is the belief that anyone who nods his head to the propositional truth of a gospel presentation and agrees to repeat the sinner's prayer after us is automatically regenerated. We have become so sure of this that we step right in after the "Amen" of the sinner's prayer is pronounced to assure whoever has prayed it with us that they are a Christian and should never doubt it. Never mind that assuring them of their salvation is the Holy Spirit's job and not ours *(Romans 8:16)*.

Too many people in our churches today have had their reservations for Heaven confirmed by us instead of by the Holy Spirit.

They believe they are saved from their sins because we have told them so. Although they have experienced the power of our persuasion through a gospel presentation, they have never experienced *"the Gospel of Christ,* [which] *is the power of God unto salvation"* *(Romans 1:16).*

Salvation is more than our persuading others to accept Christ. It is their experiencing God's life-changing power for themselves. This is why the Apostle Paul taught the Corinthians that *"the kingdom of God is not in word, but in power"* *(I Corinthians 4:20).* No matter how persuasive we are in presenting the gospel or how many sinners we persuade to pray the sinner's prayer, if God doesn't do something in the sinner's life, salvation never occurs.

The Apostle Paul understood that salvation is not a simple matter of sinners coming under the persuasive power of Christians. It is the weightier matter of sinners experiencing the life-changing power of Jesus Christ. This is why Paul refused to use *"excellency of speech"* or *"enticing words of man's wisdom"* in his preaching *(I Corinthians 2:1–5).* Paul intentionally limited his preaching of the gospel to *"Jesus Christ, and him crucified."* He did this so that his converts, unlike so many of ours today, would not turn to Christ under the power of human persuasion but only under *"the power of God."* Paul wanted his preaching to be a *"demonstration of the Spirit and of the power"* of God. He did not want his preaching to be a demonstration of his eloquence, cleverness, and persuasiveness.

It Takes A Miracle

Our God is a miracle working God. He divided the Red Sea. He caused the sun to stand still. He invaded our world as a human infant through the womb of a virgin named Mary. He lived a miraculous life as a man. He died on the cross for our sins and then rose from the dead on the third day. Afterward, He ascended into Heaven and promised to come back again.

All of these miracles, as well as every other miracle of God, have been performed by God to make the greatest of all miracles possible. What is God's greatest miracle? It is the miracle of salvation that He works in the lives of unworthy sinners like you and me. As John Peterson wrote:

> *"It took a miracle to put the stars in place,*
> *It took a miracle to hang the world in space;*
> *But when He saved my soul,*
> *Cleansed and made me whole,*
> *It took a miracle of love and grace."*[2]

Salvation is a miracle of God. It is not, as we are prone to say, "So simple that a little child can understand it." Rather, it is so stupendous that only a miracle working God can perform it! Until we realize this truth, we will never fully appreciate our salvation, nor will we truly understand the urgent need the lost have for our prayers.

The lost stand in desperate need of our prayers. Only God can perform the miracle of salvation on their behalf. They may pray the sinner's prayer, and we may present the gospel to them, but it still takes a miracle of God for a sinner to be saved. Therefore, we must cry out to God day and night, asking Him to do for sinners what only He can. After all, He is *"the Lord; and* [apart from Him] *there is no saviour" (Isaiah 43:11).*

THE RICH YOUNG RULER

In Mark 10:17–27, we are told about our Lord's encounter with the rich young ruler. The rich young ruler had everything the world has to offer. He was young; therefore, we may assume that he was healthy and strong, possessing the vitality of youth. He had the promise of a bright future before him. He was also rich as Mark points out in verse 22: *"He had great possessions."* He was a man with the means to buy whatever his heart desired. Furthermore, he was a ruler, a man with great power. He held a high position and enjoyed the prominence and popularity associated with such standing in the world.

In spite of having everything the world has to offer, the rich young ruler still wasn't satisfied. The reason for this is that the world cannot satisfy. Have you ever noticed how unsatisfying the things of the world are? Who are the ones most unsatisfied with this world's possessions? Is it not those who possess the most? Is it not the rich who are most unsatisfied with riches? No matter how rich they are, they appear ever driven to accumulate more and more riches, and no matter how much they accumulate, they are never satisfied with the riches they have.

The same can be said of fame that is said of fortune; those who possess the most of it appear least satisfied with it. No matter how many standing ovations celebrities receive, they are never satisfied. They appear ever driven to another curtain call, and no matter how much applause they hear, they must always hear more and more.

Who are the most power-hungry people in this world? Is it not those who are already in power? No matter what office they hold, they appear ever driven to higher office, and no matter how high their office or how long they've held it, they are never satisfied with the power they possess.

Who is more unsatisfied with drink than the drunkard? Who is more unsatisfied with food than the glutton? Who is more unsatisfied with sensual pleasure than the sexually promiscuous? On and on we could go, but I believe the point is proven. This world cannot satisfy the hungry soul; only God can *(Psalm 107:9)*. This is why the rich young ruler came to Jesus. He hoped that Jesus could do for him what the world never could—satisfy his hungry soul.

HOW THE RICH YOUNG RULER CAME TO CHRIST

We now know why the rich young ruler came to Christ, but have we ever considered how he came? How he came is most intriguing, especially in the light of how he went away. The rich young ruler did all of the things that we say one has to do to be saved; nevertheless, he went away lost.

Notice, first of all, that the rich young ruler came to Christ publicly. He came *"when Christ was gone forth into the way" (verse 17)*. Many in evangelical churches view one's public profession of Christ synonymously with one's actual possession of Christ. This, in spite of Jesus' words in Matthew 7:21, *"Not everyone that saith unto me, Lord, Lord, shall enter into the kingdom of heaven; but he that doeth the will of my father which is in heaven."*

As the story of the rich young ruler attests, not everyone who comes to Christ publicly is saved. Many lost people have walked the church aisle and gone forward in a church service. They have made a public decision for Christ; however, they have never become a disciple of Christ. Their name may have been added to the church's membership roll, but it has never been recorded in the Lamb's book of life *(Revelation 21:27)*.

Not only did the rich young ruler come to Christ publicly, but he also came praying. He *"kneeled"* before Christ and asked *"Good Master, what shall I do that I may inherit eternal life" (verse 17)*. Many evangelicals believe that anyone who prays the sinner's prayer and asks Christ for eternal life is automatically regenerated. They are so certain of this that they assure everyone who prays the sinner's prayer that he is a shoo-in for Heaven. Consequently, many sinners, who bear no resemblance to the Heavenly Father, insist that they are His children just because they once prayed the sinner's prayer and were welcomed into God's family by some well-meaning but misguided Christian.

Have you ever met people who guarantee you that they are saved by God's grace even though they appear to be completely ignoring God's will for their life? They may have the most lascivious of lifestyles. They may not remember the last time they darkened the door of a church, cracked the back on a Bible, or bowed their head in prayer. Nevertheless, they are sure of their salvation simply because they "prayed the prayer" when they were eight years old in Vacation Bible School.

In Matthew 7:22–23, Jesus presents the fearful prospect that one could be clinging to a false assurance of salvation even on Judgment Day. According to Jesus, *"many...in that day"* who have never met Him will still be insisting that they know Him. They will attempt to prove their acquaintance with Christ by what they have done, namely their preaching of the gospel, their casting out of devils, and their performing of many wonderful works.

If the only evidence we have of salvation is something that we ourselves have done, rest assured that it will not standup under Christ's scrutiny on the Day of Judgment. When we individually stand before Christ, we better have some proof to present from our lives that God has done something. If all one has to show for his salvation is a prayer he prayed when he was eight years old, I'm afraid he, too, will hear Christ say, *"I never knew you: depart from me, ye that work iniquity."*

Along with praying and coming publicly, the rich young ruler also came to Christ believing. He believed that Jesus was who He claimed to be. This is evidenced by the fact that he called Christ *"Good Master."* He also believed that Christ could give him *"eternal life,"* which explains why he came to Jesus requesting it.

Many people presume that salvation is nothing more than believing the facts about Jesus. They are persuaded that anyone who intellectually commits to all the Scripture says about the Savior is automatically saved. To them being a Christian is merely consenting to the claims of Christ—nothing more than nodding a head to everything the Bible teaches.

The Scripture issues to us the following warning in James 2:19: *"Thou believest that there is one God; thou doest well: the devils also believe, and tremble."* The devil believes in God. He knows that Jesus is the Son of God. He knows that Jesus was born of a virgin. He knows that Jesus lived a miraculous life. He knows that Jesus died on the cross for the sins of the world. He knows that Jesus rose from the dead. He knows that Jesus ascended into Heaven. He knows that Jesus is coming back again. Still, in spite of this, the devil is no Christian.

Believing the truth about Jesus Christ will no more make a person a Christian than it does the devil. This is the whole point that James was making. This in no way should downplay the importance of believing the truth about Jesus Christ. No one can ever be a Christian who doesn't believe it. Still, believing the truth about Jesus Christ is not sufficient in and of itself to save one from his sins as is proven by Christ's encounter with the rich young ruler. Although the rich young ruler believed the truth about Jesus, he still went away lost.

SPURIOUS FAITH

Did you know that the Bible speaks about a spurious faith? Not all faith is saving faith. According to the Bible, it is possible to possess a faith that falls far short of salvation.

In our Lord's parable of the sower, He tells how some of the seed is sown *"upon a rock" (Luke 8:6)*. Later, when asked by His disciples about the parable, Jesus explains that the seed *"on the rock are they, which, when they hear, receive the word with joy; and these have no root, which for a while believe, and in time of temptation fall away"* (Luke 8:13). Notice, these spurious believers not only *"hear"* and *"receive the word with joy,"* but they also *"believe"* at least for awhile. Their faith soon fails them, however, when it is put to the test *"in a time of temptation."* Why do they *"fall away?"* It is because theirs is a spurious faith that falls far short of salvation.

In John 2:23–25, we are told about the spurious faith of *"many"* who were in Jerusalem to observe the Passover. According to John, these Jews believed on Jesus, *"when they saw the miracles which he did."* Despite their faith, Jesus refused to *"commit himself unto them, because he knew all men."* What was it about the faith of these believers that kept Christ at a distance from them? Was it not the fact that Jesus *"knew what was in man"*? He knew that their faith was spurious. Hence, He refused to *"commit himself unto them."* He only commits Himself unto those with saving faith.

In Acts 8:9–24, we are told about the spurious faith of Simon the sorcerer. Simon not only *"believed"* but was also "baptized." Shortly afterward, he was condemned by the Apostle Peter for still being *"in the gall of bitterness, and in the bond of iniquity."* How could this be? Did Simon lose his salvation shortly after receiving it? Absolutely not! One cannot lose what he never had. Simon was never saved to start with. His was a spurious faith, not saving faith.

The Apostle Paul warned the Corinthians about the danger of *"believing in vain"* (1 Corinthians 15:2). As one who believed all the Scripture before his conversion, Paul understood the danger of possessing a faith that falls far short of salvation. Perhaps, this is why he admonishes us to *"examine ourselves"* and *"prove ourselves"* as to *"whether"* or not *"we are in the faith"* *(2 Corinthians 13:5)*.

How The Rich Young Ruler Went Away

When we add the rich young ruler's morality and religious upbringing *(Mark 10:19–20)* to the fact that he did everything we say one has to do to be saved, it truly becomes inconceivable that he went away lost. Unlike Christ, today's evangelicals would not have stood silently and watched the rich young ruler walk away *"sad"* and *"grieved."* Instead, we would have assured him of his salvation, welcomed him into God's family, and extended to him the right hand of church fellowship. Christ, on the other hand, refused to lower the bar of salvation for anyone. By standing silently and watching the rich young ruler walk away, Christ preached to us all a most powerful message.

As the disciples stood with Christ and watched the rich young ruler walk away they *"were astonished out of measure, saying among themselves, 'Who then can be saved?'"* *(verse 26)*. If someone like the rich young ruler cannot be saved by coming to Christ publicly, believing in Christ personally, and kneeling before Christ prayerfully, then who can? If those who have all the world, religion, and morality have to offer cannot be saved by coming to Christ in prayer, in faith, and in public, then what hope do you and I have? No wonder Christ's disciples began murmuring among themselves.

In response to the disciples' bewilderment, Jesus replied, *"With men it* [salvation] *is impossible"* *(verse 27)*. It is impossible for us to do anything to save ourselves. We cannot save ourselves by making a decision for Christ. We cannot save ourselves by publicly professing our faith in Christ. We cannot save ourselves by praying the sinner's prayer. We cannot save ourselves by nodding our head to the propositional truth of a gospel presentation. We cannot even save ourselves by observing the Ten Commandments. There is simply nothing we can ever do to save ourselves.

In light of the fact that salvation is impossible with men, we should be eternally grateful to God for that little conjunction *"but"* in *Mark 10:27*. Jesus said, *"With men it is impossible, but not with God."* According to Jesus, *"with God all things are possible,"* even our salvation. Thank God that He can do for us what we cannot possibly do for ourselves. He alone can save us from our sins. Though our salvation is utterly impossible without God, it is entirely possible with Him.

Until this truth sinks deep into our souls, I seriously doubt that we will ever understand the plight of the lost or their desperate need for our prayers. There is nothing between a lost soul and a Christless eternity than one second of time. There is no possibility of the lost soul's salvation apart from a miracle of God. Without God's performance of the impossible, our unsaved loved ones, friends, and acquaintances are hopelessly and eternally lost.

The plight of the lost and their desperate need of our prayers should continuously drive us into our prayer closets. From there, we should cry out to Heaven day and night for those whom God has burdened us. The eternities of lost souls are hanging in the balance, but a sovereign God has chosen to tip the scales in their favor through our prayers. The prayers we offer from burdened hearts will be used by God to alter eternal destinies. What other incentive do we need to spend the rest of our lives in prayer for the lost?

PRAYER

"You are the Lord, and apart from you, there is no Savior. I thank you that all things are possible with you, even man's salvation. For this greatest of all your miracles, the miracle of salvation, I shall forever praise your holy name.

I now drop to my knees under the weight of the burden you have given me for the lost. I pray that you will work the miracle of salvation on their behalf. Please have mercy on their souls, for apart from your performance of the impossible on their behalf, they shall forever remain hopelessly and helplessly lost. Amen."

Chapter 8
THE GIFT OF FAITH

After reading the last chapter, you may be wondering just how much you have to do with your own salvation. The answer may shock and surprise you. According to the Bible, man has nothing to do with his salvation. Salvation is completely of God.

Today's commonly held view of salvation is that we have our part to play and God has His. If we do our part, God is then duty-bound to do His part. Therefore, our salvation is supposedly up to us. It only awaits our willingness to do our part. Once our part is done, God does His, and salvation is ours.

According to this popular view of salvation, the devil has voted against us, God has voted for us, and we have the deciding vote. The Bible teaches, however, that we are not even registered voters, thanks to our total depravity and spiritual bankruptcy. When it comes to election, God's eternal choice of individuals unto salvation, neither the devil nor we have a vote. It is God alone who elects those who shall be saved *(Psalm 65:4)*.

In today's pulpits, God is often portrayed as wringing His hands in Heaven while all-powerful man decides what to do about his own salvation. Such a portrayal of God may be worse than error. It may be blasphemy. To preach that we are the deciding factor in our own salvation is hubris. What greater exhibition of pride could we possibly perpetrate against the Almighty?

The Bible plainly teaches that our *"boasting...is excluded"* from God's salvation of our souls *(Romans 3:27)*. Even the Apostle Paul, arguably the greatest Christian who ever lived, said he had nothing to boast about except *"the cross of the Lord Jesus Christ" (Galatians 6:14)*. Contrary to this, today's commonly held view of salvation leaves us with a great deal to boast about. If we play the deciding role in our salvation or any role at all for that matter, we can spend eternity strutting up and down Heaven's golden streets.

Besides giving us bragging rights, today's popular view of salvation also attributes to us certain things that we are completely incapable of performing. What is popularly considered today as our part in salvation is actually no less God's doing than the rest of our salvation. A careful study of God's Word will prove this to any open-minded individual.

That the Bible teaches we must do certain things to be saved is irrefutable. For instance, none of us would argue with the fact that the Bible teaches we must believe in the Lord Jesus Christ and repent of our sins in order to be saved. The question comes, however, with our capacity to do these things. Are we capable of believing in Christ and repenting of our sins whenever we choose to do so?

The Scripture teaches that we are spiritually impotent and impoverished. Consequently, we are totally incapable of doing anything the Bible says we must do to be saved. We cannot work up within ourselves a saving faith in the Lord Jesus Christ; neither can we grit our teeth and make ourselves repent of our sins. There is simply no way that we can pull ourselves up by our own boot-straps and make ourselves do any of the things that the Bible says we must do to be saved.

Since we cannot do what the Bible says we must do to be saved, Christ has to step in and do it for us. Without His interven-tion we cannot possibly do it ourselves. Thus, what is mistakenly believed to be our part in salvation is just as much Christ's doing as the rest of our salvation. Our salvation is completely His doing. We have nothing to do with it. Christ has to do it all for us because we are incapable of doing any of it ourselves.

The Gift Of Faith

We all know that no one can be saved without believing in the Lord Jesus Christ. When the Philippian jailer asked the Apostle Paul what he needed to do to be saved, Paul answered, *"Believe on the Lord Jesus Christ, and thou shalt be saved" (Acts 16:31)*. This certainly sounds simple enough. It sounds so simple that most of the church has concluded that anybody can be saved at any-time and that all a person has to do is believe.

Salvation by faith is not as simple as it sounds. It is definitely not as simple as most Christians make it out to be. In Ephesians 2:8–9, the Apostle Paul writes: *"For by grace are ye saved through faith; and that not of yourselves: it is the gift of God: Not of works, lest any man should boast."* Notice, Paul says that the very faith we exercise to be saved by God's grace is *"not of ourselves: it is the gift of God."* According to Paul, saving faith is not something we can work up within ourselves anytime we take a notion. Instead, it is a gift of God. God must give it to us.

Where does faith come from? The Bible says, *"Faith cometh by hearing and hearing by the Word of God" (Romans 10:17)*. There are two Greek words for *"word."* One is *"logos,"* which means *"the written word."* The other is *"rhema,"* which means *"the spoken word."* The Greek word used in Romans 10:17 is *"rhema"* not *"logos."*

Many people misinterpret Romans 10:17. They believe it says, *"Faith cometh by reading and reading by the Bible."* Pastors often wave the Bible while quoting Romans 10:17. They preach that the Bible is the source of faith. Despite the popularity of this misinterpretation of Paul's teaching, faith does not come from reading the Bible or from biblical exposition.

I know atheists who have read the Bible through several times. In spite of this, they still remain faithless. There are unbelievers in our churches who have set under the preaching of the Bible for years, yet like the *"silly women"* Paul spoke about to Timothy, these unbelieving church members are *"ever learning, and never able to come to the knowledge of the truth" (2 Timothy 3:6–7)*.

Faith doesn't come from reading the written Word of God or from hearing it preached or taught. Faith comes *"from hearing"* the spoken *"Word of God."* Faith is never born in people's hearts until they hear God's Spirit speak His Word directly and personally to them. Granted, God's Spirit may speak His Word to our heart while we are reading the Bible or hearing it preached. Still, it is hearing God not reading the Bible or hearing the preacher that produces faith.

The faith we exercise to be saved by God's grace must be given to us by God. God gives it to us by quickening the written word off of the page and making it come alive in our hearts. Once the Holy Spirit transforms the written word into the spoken word by speaking it directly and personally to us, faith is born in our hearts. We can then—and only then—be saved by God's grace through faith in God's Son.

God must speak His Word to our hearts if we are ever to believe and be saved. Therefore, faith is, as the Apostle Paul taught the Ephesians, a gift from God. It is not something we can work up within ourselves. It is something God does for us because we are incapable of believing on our own.

THE PROVOCATION

The Bible repeatedly warns us not to harden our hearts on the day we hear God's voice *(Psalm 95:7–8; Hebrews 3:7–8, 15)*. Why does the Scripture repeatedly issue this warning? Is it not because we can only come to Christ by faith when we hear God's voice? If we harden our hearts when we hear God's voice, we have no guarantee of ever hearing it again. For all we know, if we harden our hearts to the voice of God today, our coming to Christ by faith may be an impossibility tomorrow.

In warning us not to harden our hearts on the day we hear God's voice, both the Psalmist and the author of Hebrews refer to *"the provocation, in the day of temptation in the wilderness."* What is *"the provocation"*? It is Israel's provoking God to anger by hardening her heart during her time of testing in the wilderness. Although there are a number of instances that may be referred to, such as Massah and Meribah, which literally mean *"temptation"* and *"provocation,"* the author of Hebrews appears to be referring specifically to Israel's provoking of God at Kadesh-Barnea.

At Kadesh-Barnea, the Israelites hardened their hearts to God's voice and refused to do what He said, namely to enter into Canaan and take possession of it. Due to their refusal to believe Him on the day they heard His voice, God became *"grieved with that generation."* He was so grieved with them that He swore in His wrath that they would never enter into His rest *(Hebrews 3:10–11)*. The *"carcasses"* of that whole generation *"fell in the wilderness"* *(Hebrews 3:17)*. With the exceptions of Caleb and Joshua, who alone believed God, that entire generation died in the desert without ever stepping foot into Canaan.

After hardening their hearts and incurring God's wrath on the day they heard His voice, the Israelites changed their minds and decided the next day to obey God and enter Canaan *(Numbers 14:39–45)*. Against the advice of Moses, who warned them of God's withdrawal from them and the enemies' impending defeat of them, the people *"presumed"* they could still conquer Canaan. They entered the land only to be *"smitten"* by the *"Amalekites"* and *"Canaanites."* The Israelites learned, much to their own chagrin, that the voice of God can only be obeyed on the day it is heard.

The Israelite people could only enter Canaan on the day they heard God's voice. They had no hope of conquering it at any other time. Likewise, sinners can only come to salvation on the day they hear God's voice. They have no hope of believing in Christ and being saved at any other time. They may presume to come to Christ at another time, but their presumption will no more lead to salvation than Israel's did to conquest.

We need to pray that God will give the gift of faith to the lost. We need to ask God to speak His Word directly and personally to them through the person of the Holy Spirit because only then can saving faith be born in their hearts.

We also need to pray that the lost will not harden their hearts on the day that they hear God's voice. It is only on the day that they hear God's voice that the gift of faith can be given to them. Only then can the lost believe in Christ and be saved by God's grace. If they harden their hearts on the day they hear God's voice, provoking Him to anger, there is no promise that they will ever hear His voice again. There also is no guarantee that they will ever have another opportunity to be saved.

PRAYER

"I praise you, Lord Jesus, the author and finisher of my faith. I ask you to give the gift of faith to the lost for whom I am burdened. I pray that faith will be born in their hearts as you speak your Word directly and personally to them through the person of the Holy Spirit. I also pray that on the day they hear your voice they will not harden their hearts, provoking you to anger but will come to you by faith and be saved by your grace. Amen."

Don Walton

Chapter 9

THE GRANTING OF REPENTANCE

I n Acts 3:19, the Apostle Peter boldly declares, *"Repent ye therefore, and be converted, that your sins may be blotted out."* Individuals cannot *"be converted"* and have their *"sins…blotted out"* unless they *"repent."* This is the very message that Jesus commissioned his disciples to preach to the world *(Luke 24:47)*.

That repentance is a necessity for salvation is a scriptural certainty. That no one can be saved without it is indisputable. Yet, the question remains. "Are we capable of repenting in and of ourselves?" The biblical answer is a definite "No."

In Acts 5:31, the Apostle Peter told the Sanhedrin that God exalted Christ *"to be a Prince and a Saviour"* so that He could *"give repentance to Israel, and forgiveness of sins."* Later, thanks to Peter's vision at Simon's house in Joppa and subsequent visit to Cornelius' house in Caesarea, the church in Jerusalem concluded that God had also *"granted repentance unto life"* to *"the Gentiles"* *(Acts 11:18)*. Notice, repentance, like *"forgiveness of sins,"* was a gift from God to both the Jews and the Gentiles. Neither of them worked it up within themselves. It was given to them by God.

In 2 Timothy 2:25–26, the Apostle Paul taught the young minister Timothy that the only hope the youth's opposition had of ever *"acknowledging the truth"* and escaping *"out of the snare of the devil"* was if God would *"give them repentance."* Once again, repentance is presented as a gift from God. It is not something we can decide to do ourselves. It is something God must give us. Therefore, we should pray for God to grant repentance to the lost. Until He does, the lost have no hope of being converted, having their sins forgiven, acknowledging the truth, or escaping from the snare of the devil.

True And False Repentance

In 2 Corinthians 7:8–11, the Apostle Paul speaks of his assurance that the repentance of the Corinthian Christians was genuine. Just as there is a saving faith and a spurious faith, there is also a true and false repentance. *"Repentance to salvation,"* according to 2 Corinthians 7:10, comes from *"godly sorrow,"* which produces a repentance *"not to be repented of."* Conversely, repentance that falls short of salvation is produced by *"the sorrow of the world"* and results in *"death."*

The Sorrow Of The World

Esau is a good example of someone in the Bible who was sorry for his sin with *"the sorrow of the world."* The Bible says that Esau *"found no place of repentance, though he sought it carefully with tears" (Hebrews 12:16–17).* Although Esau was sorry for his sin to the point of tears, he never found the place of true repentance. How could this possibly be? How can anyone be tearfully sorry for his sin without being truly repentant?

What seems to be inexplicable is explained by the Bible's description of Esau as a *"profane person...who for one morsel of meat sold his birthright."* Esau cared nothing about the promised Messiah. He had such little regard for the coming Son of God that he swapped his place in the Savior's lineage for a bowl of stew. Afterward, he was sorry that his poor spiritual bartering had left him spiritually impoverished. Still, in spite of his *"tears,"* he never found true repentance.

Why was Esau sorry for his sin? Was it because it broke the heart of God in Heaven and would one day bloody the body of Christ on the cross? Absolutely not! Esau couldn't have cared less about this. His only concern over his sin was its consequences. He was sad because of what his sin cost him, namely his birthright and father's blessing.

The world is full of profane people like Esau, people who care nothing about Christ. They couldn't care less that their sin nailed God's Son to Calvary's cross. Their only concern over their sin is its consequences. Like Esau, they tearfully seek the *"place of repentance"* in the hope of annulling or avoiding the consequences of their sin.

Worldly sorrow never leads to the place of true repentance. Only *"godly sorrow"* can lead us there. Whereas worldly sorrow results in the shedding of tears over the consequences of sin, godly sorrow results in the actual loathing of sin itself. The truly repentant are not just disturbed by sin's consequences but find sin itself to be despicable.

THE GIFT OF TEARS

Where does godly sorrow come from? It only comes from the conviction of the Holy Spirit. In John 16:8, Jesus promised that when the Holy Spirit came *"he would reprove the world of sin."* The Holy Spirit convicts us of sin. It is He alone who breaks our hearts over our sin against God. The Puritans understood this. This is why they often prayed for *"the gift of tears."* The Puritans knew that godly sorrow, which leads to true repentance, was just as much a gift from God as the true repentance itself.

In Psalm 51:17, David speaks of the only sacrifices God desires from sinners: *"a broken spirit"* and *"a broken and contrite heart."* Having committed the odious sins of adultery and murder, David knew that the only acceptable thing he could offer God was a heart broken over his sin. Likewise, the only acceptable sacrifice sinners can offer God today is the sacrifice of a broken heart.

How can the sinful hearts of the lost ever be broken over their sin against God? Remember, we're no longer talking about worldly sorrow, being heartbroken over what our sin cost us, but godly sorrow, being heartbroken over what our sin cost Christ. How can the lost, who delight in sin, ever be brokenhearted over it? Truly, this is an impossibility apart from a miracle of God.

The "prince of preachers," Charles Spurgeon, understood that it took a divine miracle to deposit *"godly sorrow"* in sinful hearts. This is why he wrote, *"Genuine, spiritual mourning for sin is the work of the Spirit of God. Repentance is too choice a flower to grow in nature's garden. Pearls grow naturally in oysters, but penitence never shows itself in sinners except divine grace works it in them. If thou hast one particle of real hatred for sin, God must have given it thee, for human nature's thorns never produced a single fig."*[3]

In his Christian classic, "My Utmost for His Highest," Oswald Chambers writes, *"The entrance into the Kingdom is through the panging pains of repentance."* Chambers goes on to add that it is *"the Holy Spirit who produces these agonies."*[4] Truly, no one will ever find true repentance apart from the conviction of the Holy Spirit. Only the Holy Spirit can break our hearts over our sins and lead us to the place of true repentance.

REMEMBERING LOT'S WIFE

The Apostle Paul described true repentance as *"repentance to salvation not to be repented of."* True repentance is a turning away from sin and a turning to Christ that will never be turned from. All who turn back have never truly repented, nor are they fit for the kingdom of God *(Luke 9:62)*. This explains why the Apostle John wrote the following about the Christian apostates of his day: *"They went out from us, but they were not of us; for if they had been of us, they would no doubt have continued with us: but they went out, that they might be made manifest that they were not all of us"* *(1 John 2:19)*.

True repentance will never *"be repented of"* because it is more than a mere change of direction. It is a miraculous change of the human heart. Spurgeon called it *"an entire and total change of mind, a turning of the mind right around, so that it hates what it once loved and loves what it once hated."*[5] Those for whom God works the miracle of repentance will find themselves undergoing a total change of opinion and feeling in regard to sin. What they once desired, they will now detest, and what they once found alluring, they will now find abhorrent. According to the Apostle Paul, the truly repentant will be astounded that they were ever attracted to what they now find appalling *(Romans 6:21)*.

In Luke 17:32, one of Scripture's shortest verses, our Lord warns us: *"Remember Lot's wife."* Lot's wife will forever be memorialized as the epitome of false repentance. While fleeing Sodom at the command of God, Lot's wife looked back with longing eyes upon that sinful place. As a result of turning back toward Sodom, God turned her into a pillar of salt. Instead of turning from Sodom and being delivered, she ended up looking back and being destroyed.

The Apostle Peter characterizes false repentance as a *"dog* [returning] *to his own vomit"* and a washed pig to *"her wallowing in the mire" (2 Peter 2:22)*. Dogs return to their own vomit and washed pigs to their wallowing in the mud because it is their nature to do so. Likewise, those without true repentance will always return to sin because it is their nature to do so. Since they have never received from God the gift of true repentance, their sinful nature remains unchanged. With an unchanged nature, they can no more keep from looking back at sin than Lot's wife could keep from looking back at Sodom.

THE PERSEVERANCE OF THE SAINTS

Jesus said, *"But he that shall endure unto the end, the same shall be saved" (Matthew 24:13)*. Many have taken these words of our

Lord to mean that perseverance is a requirement for salvation. What our Lord really meant, however, is that perseverance is a result of salvation. We don't have to persevere to be saved, but if we are saved, we will persevere.

The perseverance of the saints is made possible by God granting them repentance. Thanks to the conviction of the Holy Spirit, the saints have been led to the place of true repentance by *"godly sorrow."* Having found the place of true repentance, the saints have discovered their natures miraculously changed by God. No longer do they find the Savior's yoke hard and His burden heavy, but they now find His yoke *"easy"* and His burden *"light" (Matthew 11:28–30)*. No longer are the commandments of Christ *"grievous"* to them, but they now *"serve the Lord with gladness" (1 John 5:3; Psalm 100:2)*.

With changed natures come changed desires. With changed desires come permanently changed lives. The saints' turning from sin is permanent because they no longer desire to practice sin. Christ has become the desire of their hearts. Therefore, they will live the rest of their lives for Him. They will *"endure unto the end."* Their perseverance is assured by their desire to please Christ.

PRAYER

"I pray, O God, that you would grant repentance to the lost for whom I am burdened so that they may acknowledge the truth, escape from the snare of the devil, be converted, and have their sins blotted out. I also pray that the Holy Spirit will convict the lost of sin and break their sinful hearts with godly sorrow, which alone produces repentance to

salvation never to be repented of. May all who find the place of true repentance persevere unto the end, proving themselves fit for the king-dom of God. Amen."

Chapter 10
THE HOUND OF HEAVEN

N o one can be saved apart from the conviction of the Holy Spirit. In spite of this, many Christians attempt to persuade the unconvicted to be converted. This is especially true in the case of children. In today's church, children are often said to be saved from their sins before they even know what sin is.

Years ago, during a pastorate in Tennessee, two small boys were brought to me during Vacation Bible School. They both had expressed an interest in asking Jesus into their hearts. As pastor of the church, I was supposed to lead these lads in the sinner's prayer, and on the following Lord's Day, I was to present them to our congregation as two trophies of God's grace won in our Bible school.

Instead of adhering to common practice, I decided that the occasion called for something unconventional. Rather than asking the boys if they wanted to invite Jesus into their hearts—I've never met a little child who didn't—I asked them if they knew what sin was. The first little boy responded, "Sin is when we do something for Jesus." The other lad quickly objected, "No it's not! Sin is how much Jesus really does love you and how much He really does care for you."

I explained to these cute youngsters that a day would come in their lives when they would know what sin was. Furthermore, they would know that they were sinners in need of a Savior. On that day, they would need to ask Jesus into their hearts. Until then, they had nothing to worry about. After all, Jesus promised that the kingdom of Heaven belongs to little children *(Matthew 19:14)*.

THE AGE OF ACCOUNTABILITY

The innocence of a child is a most fragrant flower in a fallen world. Unfortunately, it quickly withers at the age of accountability. The Bible says, *"Therefore to him that knoweth to do good, and doeth it not, to him it is sin" (James 4:17)*. There comes a time in all of our lives when we know to do good but decide to do wrong instead. At that moment, when we willfully and deliberately choose to sin, we become guilty before God. Granted, the age of accountability comes sooner for some than others. It is not something that we all celebrate on our twelfth birthday. Still, it is something that eventually comes to us all. Along with it comes the loss of our childish innocence.

As those who have lost their childish innocence, we are confronted with the peril of our lost soul. This peril puts us in desperate need of a Savior. It takes the conviction of the Holy Spirit, however, to reveal to us our dire spiritual straits. The Holy Spirit alone convicts us of sin and convinces us of our need for Christ, so without the Holy Spirit's conviction, we will never be convinced of our lost condition or our desperate need of salvation.

THE COUNSELOR

In John 16:7–11, Jesus said, *"Nevertheless I tell you the truth; It is expedient for you that I go away: for if I go not away, the Comforter will not come unto you; but if I depart, I will send him unto you. And when he is come, he will reprove the world of sin, and of righteousness, and of judgment: Of sin, because they believe not on me; Of righteousness, because I go to my Father, and ye see me no more; Of judgment, because the prince of this world is judged."* The Comforter that Jesus promised to send in this passage is the Holy Spirit. The Greek word for *"Comforter"* means *"Counselor."* In Jesus' day, this word was used in reference to legal assistants who presented, pleaded, and proved cases in court.

The coming of the Holy Spirit has put the whole world on trial for its hideous crime of crucifying Christ. The defendants in the case are this earth's inhabitants. The witnesses in the case are Christians. Remember, Jesus promised that we would be His witnesses once the Holy Spirit came *(Acts 1:8)*. The Judge is Christ Himself to whom the Father has committed all judgment *(John 5:22)*. And the prosecuting attorney, or counselor, is the Holy Spirit. The Holy Spirit has come to convince and convict this Christ-rejecting world of its crime against God.

Although we can witness for Christ, only the Holy Spirit can prove to man God's case against him. This is one of the reasons why Jesus said, *"It is expedient for you that I go away: for if I go not away, the Comforter* [Counselor] *will not come unto you."* Without the Counselor, God's case against the world cannot be proven to sinners, no matter how good the witnesses are. This explains why Jesus told His witnesses to wait in Jerusalem for the coming of the Holy Spirit *(Acts 1:4)*. Jesus knew that without the Counselor our witnessing would never result in the sinner's conviction. Only the closing argument of the Holy Spirit can persuade sinners to confess their sins and throw themselves on the mercy of the court.

CONVICTING THE WORLD OF SIN

The first thing Jesus said the Holy Spirit would convict the world of was *"sin."* Notice, Jesus did not say *"sins"* but *"sin."* There is a big difference between sins and sin. Sins are what we do. Sin is what we are. Contrary to popular opinion, man's problem is not what he does but what he is.

Most people believe that man is a sinner because he sins. Nothing, however, could be farther from the truth. Man is not a sinner because he sins; he sins because he is a sinner. A thief is not a thief because he steals; he steals because he is a thief. A liar is not a liar because he lies; he lies because he is a liar. What we do is a direct result of what we are.

The world has always shown an uncanny proficiency at separating what a man is from the things he does. For instance, when some villain commits the most hideous of crimes a desperate attempt ensues to excuse him of his evil. His evil deed is explained away by something like a troubled childhood. Thus, the villain is transformed into a victim, and the very idea that he is evil is dismissed in spite of the evil he has perpetrated. By refusing to confront the sin of evil's most notorious practitioners, our world is able to shut its eyes to the sin that lurks within us all.

Shutting our eyes to our sin by separating the things we do from what we are enables us to hold a lofty view of ourselves while committing the most loathsome acts. Our outlandish behavior is excused and our self-esteem maintained by whitewashing our misdeeds with statements like: "I'm just not myself today," "I don't know what came over me," "I don't know what made me do that," or "That's just not like me." These statements and a host of others are merely attempts on our part to distance ourselves from our actions. The more space we are able to put between ourselves and our actions, the easier it becomes to believe in our own goodness despite the bad things we do.

The Bible inseparably links our sins to our sin. No one taught the indissoluble linkage between what we are and what we do more clearly than Christ. In Mark 7:18–23, Jesus said:

Are ye so without understanding also? Do ye not perceive, that whatsoever thing from without entereth into the man, it cannot defile him; Because it entereth not into his heart…That which cometh out of the man, that defileth the man. For from within, out of the heart of men, proceed evil thoughts, adulteries, fornications, murders, thefts, covetousness, wickedness, deceit, lasciviousness, an evil eye, blasphemy, pride, foolishness: All these evil things come from within, and defile the man.

According to Jesus, our problem is heart trouble. What is wrong with us is not so much the sins we commit as it is the sinful heart from which they proceed. Our sinful hearts are described in Jeremiah 17:9 as being *"deceitful above all things, and desperately wicked."* This notion of our hearts being wicked and us being depraved, though unquestionably taught in Scripture, is totally unacceptable to our world. Our world—enamored with the "I'm okay, you're okay" absurdity—is not about to embrace the scriptural truth of man's total depravity, regardless of how emphatically it is stated in a passage like Romans 3:10–18. Here, the Bible shatters all hope of our inherent goodness by offering the following synopsis of our fallen race:

There is none righteous, no, not one: There is none that under-standeth, there is none that seeketh after God. They are all gone out of the way, they are together become unprofitable; there is none that doeth good, no, not one. Their throat is an open sepul-chre; with their tongues they have used deceit; the poison of asps is under their lips: Whose mouth is full of cursing and bitterness: Their feet are swift to shed blood: Destruction and misery are in their ways: And the way of peace have they not known: There is no fear of God before their eyes.

With such an unflattering portrait of our total depravity hanging in the gallery of Scripture, how can we ever hope to paint ourselves up attractively? Without a doubt, there is no way to touch up this portrait of us painted by the inspired brush of the Apostle Paul. We may attempt to whitewash it by separating our sins from our sin, but in the end, our true colors always bleed through. We simply can't escape the truth about ourselves.

The Holy Spirit uses our sins as evidence in His case against us. With them, He is able to prove, beyond any reasonable doubt, that we are sinners. Although our sins do not make us sinners, they do prove that we are sinners. Our problem is not so much our actions as it is ourselves. It is not so much the wrong things that we do but the fact that there is something horribly wrong with the way we are. What's wrong with us is sin, and it takes the Holy Spirit to convince us of it and convict us for it.

THE SUPREME SIN

The clincher in the Holy Spirit's case against man's sin is the fact that man refuses to believe in Christ. Jesus said that the

Holy Spirit would be able to convict men *"of sin, because they believe not on me."* There is no greater proof of the sinfulness of man than his rejection of the Lord Jesus Christ. All the proof one will ever need of the blackness of man's heart is provided for you by the torn and bloody figure of Christ on the cross of Calvary. What other explanation is there for such a dark deed except the indescribable wickedness of the human heart?

The sin of unbelief is the supreme sin. It is the sin behind all other sins. Why do men sin by seeking satisfaction apart from God? Is it not because they doubt that God can satisfy? Why do men choose their own way over God's way? Is it not because they do not believe God's way is best? And why do men disobey the Word of God? Is it not because they distrust God's Word? Truly, the sin of unbelief underlies all other sins.

Some will argue that the unpardonable sin—the blasphemy against the Holy Ghost—is the supreme sin *(Mark 3:28–29)*. However, a proper understanding of the blasphemy against the Holy Ghost will reveal that this unpardonable sin is nothing more than the sin of unbelief carried to its ultimate extreme. The only sin that is unforgivable to God is unbelief. Men go to Hell for no other reason than their failure to believe in Christ.

Far from viewing it as the supreme sin against God, unbelievers often fail to see their unbelief as a sin at all. They even justify their rejection of the person and work of Jesus Christ on the grounds of their own goodness. They love to enumerate such things as their good citizenship, community involvement, and charitable contributions. Convinced of their good deeds and morals, they presume themselves to be acceptable to God, though they are without Christ. They smugly commend themselves to the Almighty on the basis of their own merits—totally oblivious to the fact that nothing is more offensive to God than such a haughty spirit.

According to Hebrews 10:29, these so-called good people who reject Christ *"hath trodden under foot the Son of God, and hath counted the blood of the covenant, wherewith* [they] *are sanctified, an unholy thing, and hath done despite unto the Spirit of grace."* In other words, they are trampling the precious blood of Jesus under their feet as a worthless thing and turning their nose up at God's offer of grace. As far as they're concerned, Jesus' death on the cross for their salvation was unnecessary. They don't need the gift of God, which *"is eternal life through Jesus Christ our Lord" (Romans 6:23).* They're persuaded that they can earn their own salvation without stooping to accept any nail-scarred handout.

Is there any wonder that Hebrews 10:27 assures unbelievers that all they have to look forward to is *"a certain fearful looking for of judgment and fiery indignation, which shall devour the adversaries?"* Oh, what *"a fearful thing"* it will be for all who reject Christ *"to fall into the hands of the living God" (Hebrews 10:31)*! What could be more frightening than standing before Christ at the Judgment with the soles of one's feet stained with His blood?

CONVICTING THE WORLD OF RIGHTEOUSNESS

The second thing Jesus said the Holy Spirit would convict the world of was *"righteousness."* What does it take for us to be right with God? What does God require? The requirements for right-eousness are found in God's Law. The Law is the standard we must live up to if we hope to live in right standing with God.

According to the Apostle Paul, God's Law requires perfect obedience on all points *(Galatians 3:10)*. James adds that the slightest infraction of any part leaves one as guilty before God as if that person had broken the entire Law *(James 2:10)*. Such a high standard of sinless perfection is far too lofty for sinners to achieve. For this reason, the Apostle Paul teaches us in Romans 3:20 and Galatians 2:16 that none of us have any hope of ever being right with God by living up to the Law.

In spite of the impossibility of sinners living sinless lives, our fallen world still believes it can satisfy God with its own right-eousness. Little does it know that our best efforts at righteous-ness are no better than *"filthy rags"* in the sight of God *(Isaiah 64:6)*. Our faith in the *"filthy rags"* of our own righteousness keeps us from our only hope of righteousness, which is being made right with God through faith in Christ *(Romans 3:22; Philippians 3:9)*. As long as we're content trying to live up to God's Law in the rags of our own righteousness, we'll never trust Christ to clothe us in His seamless robe of perfect righteousness.

At Christ's baptism and again at His transfiguration, God the Father announced, *"This is my beloved Son, in whom I am well pleased"* (Matthew 3:17, 17:5). Only the Son pleases the Father, for He alone has lived up to the Law by living a sinless life. The Scripture says that Christ *"knew no sin"* (2 Corinthians 5:21), *"did no sin" (1 Peter 2:22),* and *"was without sin" (Hebrews 4:15).* As the only sinless one, Christ alone has fulfilled the righteous requirements of God's Law *(Matthew 3:15, 5:17).*

How do we know that Christ has satisfied the righteous requirements of God's Law? According to Romans 4:25, Christ's resurrection proves that we can be "justified," or made right with God, by believing in Jesus. The resurrection is God the Father's stamp of approval on everything His Son did in our stead. If God the Father had not been satisfied with Christ, He would have never raised Him from the dead.

Now that Christ has fulfilled all righteousness for us because we could not do so for ourselves, all that remains for us to do is to accept by faith what Christ has done. When we do, Christ becomes *"our righteousness" (1 Corinthians 1:30),* and we become *"accepted* [by God] *in the beloved" (Ephesians 1:6).* We become right with God not because of anything we have done but because of everything Christ has done for us.

The only way we will ever be righteous is by believing in the only one who "is righteous," God's beloved Son. Jesus said that the Holy Spirit would be able to convict the world *"of righteousness, because I go to the Father, and ye see me no more."* What greater proof is there that the Son has fulfilled all righteousness than His ascension to the right hand of the Father? Christ's exaltation by the Father proves the Father's acceptance of all His Son has done for our salvation. It also proves that there is no other way for us to be right with God except through faith in *"Jesus Christ the righteous" (I John 2:1).*

CONVICTING THE WORLD OF JUDGMENT

The final thing Jesus said the Holy Spirit would convict the world of was *"judgment."* Many people have convinced themselves that a loving God will never judge anyone. That God is loving is indisputable. The Bible teaches that God's love for us is beyond doubt, having been proven by Christ's death on the cross *(Romans 5:8; 1 John 4:9–10)*. The Bible also teaches that God's love is beyond knowledge. According to the Apostle Paul, no man can scale the heights, fathom the depths, or span the breath of *"the love of Christ, which passeth knowledge" (Ephesians 3:18–19)*.

Notwithstanding God's incomprehensible love for us, there is still the very real danger of His judgment upon us. The Bible speaks more about God's wrath and judgment than it does His love and forgiveness. Jesus spoke more about Hell than He did about Heaven. In fact, Jesus spoke more about Hell than anyone else in the Bible.

The Bible teaches that God is just. Being just, God must judge sin despite His love for the sinner. He cannot let one sin slip by unpunished or unpaid for. If He did He would cease to be just. For this reason, God is meticulously unsparing in His judgment of sin.

THE UNSPARING GOD

Both Peter and Jude warn us about the unsparing God *(2 Peter 2:4–9; Jude 5–7)*. According to them, God did not spare the angels who sinned, the prediluvian world, the cities of Sodom and Gomorrah, or even His own people when they rebelled against Him. Why then should we believe that God will spare today's Christ-rejecting world? If He did, He would have to apologize to Sodom and Gomorrah.

That God will allow no sin to go unpunished is proven by the fact that He *"spared not his own Son, but delivered him up for us all" (Romans 8:32)*. When Christ died on the cross, He suffered the full brunt of judgment for every sin that man has committed in the past, is committing in the present, or will commit in the future. God the Father held back nothing but unsparingly poured out on His Son the full fury of His wrath for all the sins of all time.

It was God's refusal to spare His own Son that makes it possible for Him to spare sinners like you and me. The only reason we can be forgiven of our sins and escape judgment is because God judged Jesus in our place when He died for our sins on the cross of Calvary. However, the author of Hebrews points out, *"How shall we escape* [God's judgment of our sin] *if we neglect so great* [a] *salvation" (Hebrews 2:3)*. Any sinner who rejects the Savior's supreme sacrifice for our sins will surely stand before the unsparing God in judgment.

The death of Christ on the cross proves God's love for sinners. It also proves God's hatred of sin. Though it speaks of the possibility of salvation, it also cries out to us of the certainty of judgment. If God hates sin so much that He spared not His own Son, what hope does our Christ-rejecting world have of escaping the wrath of God?

CONDEMNED ALREADY

According to Jesus, the Holy Spirit is able to convict the world *"of judgment, because the prince of this world is judged."* Satan, *"the prince of this world,"* is already judged. He has already been convicted and sentenced *(John 12:31; Hebrews 2:14;* and *I John 3:8).* All that awaits him is the carrying out of his execution, for his condemnation has already sealed his fate.

In John 3:18, Jesus said, *"He that believeth on* [me] *is not condemned: but he that believeth not is condemned already, because he hath not believed in the name of the only begotten Son of God."* Like Satan, the unbelieving sinner is already condemned. Far from escaping the judgment of God, the unbeliever is already under it, *"because he hath not believed in the name of the only begotten Son of God."* All the sinner awaits is the carrying out of his sentence, for his condemnation, too, has already sealed his fate.

In his famous sermon, "Sinners in the Hands of an Angry God," Jonathan Edwards speaks of the precarious predicament of sinners when he states: *"They are already under a sentence of condemnation to hell. They do not only justly deserve to be cast down thither, but the sentence of...God...is gone out against them, and stands against them; so that they are bound over already to hell."*[6]

The question unbelievers need to ask themselves is not whether a loving God will sentence them to Hell for their rejection of His Son Jesus Christ. According to Jesus, God already has! The question sinners need to consider is when will God execute His sentence against them. Again, consider the words of Jonathan Edwards:

O sinner, consider the fearful danger you are in! It is a great furnace of wrath, a wide and bottomless pit, full of the fire of wrath that you are held over in the hand of that God whose wrath is provoked against you. You hang by a slender thread, with the flames of divine wrath flashing about it and ready every moment to singe it, and burn it asunder; and you have no interest in any Mediator, and nothing to lay hold of to save yourself nothing to keep off the flames of wrath, nothing of your own, nothing that you have done, nothing that you can do, to induce God to spare you one moment.[7]

In convicting the world of judgment, the Holy Spirit convinces the unbeliever of his precarious predicament. He reveals to the sinner that his trial is over, his guilty verdict rendered, and his sentence pronounced. All that is pending is God's execution of the sinner's sentence, which could occur at any moment. Any day could be execution day.

THE HOUND OF HEAVEN

In the title of his famous poem, Francis Thompson dubbed the Holy Spirit "The Hound of Heaven."[8] Thompson's poem tells of the Holy Spirit's pursuit of him throughout his life. It concludes with the Holy Spirit driving him into the arms of God. This is the purpose for which the Holy Spirit dogs the heels of sinners. He came into the world to drive them into the arms of infinite love. His all-important mission is fulfilled by His *"convicting the world of sin, and of righteousness, and of judgment."*

PRAYER

"O God, I pray that you will unleash the Hound of Heaven on the lost for whom I am burdened. May He convict them of the guilt of their sin, of the filthy rags of their own righteousness, and of the fearful judgment already executed against them by an angry God. May He dog their heels night and day until He drives them from their sin into the loving arms of our Savior. Amen."

Chapter 11
THE UNPARDONABLE SIN

I n Genesis 6:3, the Lord said, *"My spirit shall not always strive with man."* God's patience is not, as many believe, inexhaustible. Three times in the first chapter of Romans, we read, *"God gave them up" (Romans 1:24, 26, 28)*. Men can become reprobate. When they do, *"God gives them over to* [their] *reprobate mind"* This means that the Spirit of God ceases to strive with them. Consequently, the fate of their soul is sealed and all hope of salvation forfeited.

Contrary to popular opinion, we cannot be saved anytime we choose. This fact is illustrated for us in John 6:15. The multitude, due to Christ's feeding of the five thousand, decided to force Jesus to be their king. Jesus, however, withdrew Himself from them. Jesus Christ cannot be forced to do anything. A person can no more force Jesus to be his Savior than the multitude succeeded in forcing Him to be their king.

Too many people today think they have salvation all figured out. They don't want to bother with Christ until they finish sowing their wild oats. They figure to finish strewing their life with sin around age ninety nine. Then, right before the sheet is pulled up over their head, they plan on whistling for Christ to come and save them. Believing that Christ is forced to save all who ask for salvation, these sly sinners are plotting to slip off of their deathbeds into Heaven despite living lives of debauchery.

The plot of these future deathbed confessors is fatally flawed. Its deadly error is found in the fact that Christ doesn't come to us whenever we say. On the contrary, we must come to Christ whenever God says. In John chapter 6, Jesus declared, *"No man can come to me, except the Father which hath sent me draw him" (verse 44).* In verse 65, Jesus added, *"No man can come unto me, except it were given unto him of my Father."* Salvation is only possible when God says so. It is not something to be had whenever the sinner says.

THE UNPARDONABLE SIN

In Matthew chapter 12, some Pharisees attribute Jesus' power over the demonic to *"Beelzebub the prince of devils."* In response to such hardness of heart, Jesus points out the absurdity of *"Satan casting out Satan."* He then issues this solemn warning to the hard-hearted:

> *Wherefore I say unto you, All manner of sin and blasphemy shall be forgiven unto men: but the blasphemy against the Holy Ghost shall not be forgiven unto men. And whosoever speaketh a word against the Son of man, it shall be forgiven him: but whosoever speaketh against the Holy Ghost, it shall not be forgiven him, neither in this world, neither in the world to come (Matthew 12:31–32).*

The Holy Spirit is God's final call to lost humanity. In the past, God sent His prophets to man, but man persecuted them. Then God sent His Son, but man crucified Him. Finally, God has sent the Holy Spirit into the world. The Holy Spirit is God's final invitation to fallen man. If man hardens his heart to the Spirit's invitation to come to Christ, there remains no further hope of salvation, for the sinner has committed the unforgivable.

Each time the sinner says "No" to the Spirit makes it that much easier to say "No" the next time. The sinner's heart becomes harder and harder, eventually becoming so calloused that the sinner no longer feels the Spirit's conviction. When the heart becomes calloused, the Spirit ceases His striving, and the sinner crosses God's deadline. All hope is lost. The unpardonable sin is committed!

The Devil's Greatest Wile

In Ephesians 6:11, the Apostle Paul warns us about *"the wiles of the devil."* Perhaps, the devil's greatest wile is "wait awhile." The devil will never walk up to our lost loved ones and friends and ask them to sign over their immortal souls. He's much too subtle for that. Instead, he simply seeks to persuade them to procrastinate, assuring them that there's plenty of time to respond to the Spirit's invitation. Once convinced by the devil that there's no urgency in the Spirit's conviction, the sinner is well on his way to a calloused heart.

This soul stealing strategy of Satan was brought home to me years ago in a most unforgettable way. While visiting in a nursing home, I was asked by the staff to call upon a patient. The staff informed me that this particular patient was the most tormented soul they had ever encountered; they hoped I might be able to help him.

Entering the room, I found an elderly man dressed in his street clothes and sitting in a chair. Unlike many of the other patients, this man was in control of all his faculties. I quickly learned that his lack of family had more to do with him being there than his lack of health. After a few moments of small talk, I turned our conversation to spiritual things. This appeared to prick the man's interest and heighten his attention. Encouraged by such a response I proceeded to present to him the claims of Christ.

After presenting Christ to him, I asked if he believed what I had shared. He immediately responded in the affirmative. I then asked if he would like to call upon the name of the Lord and be saved *(Romans 10:13)*. He answered, "More than anything else in the world." Nevertheless, when I encouraged him to do so he refused, insisting that it was too late for him. In my youthful exuberance, not to mention biblical ignorance, I assured him that it was never too late. To this the old man gently but sternly replied, "Young man, salvation is not a mere matter of you calling out to God. It is also a matter of God calling you. For years, God called me to come to Christ through the conviction of the Holy Spirit, but for years I answered, 'No, no, a thousand times no.' Finally, the Spirit stopped convicting my calloused heart. My problem today is not that I don't want to call upon the name of the Lord, but that the Lord no longer calls upon me!"

Had this man committed the unpardonable sin? I don't know. All I know is I felt a chill and eerie presence in that room I have never experienced before or since. I walked out leaving him as I had found him—a tormented soul.

PRAYER

"Dear Lord, I praise you for your longsuffering. I thank you for sending the Holy Spirit to call lost humanity to Christ. I pray that your Spirit will not cease to strive with the lost souls for whom I am burdened. May the urgent need of their immediate response to the Spirit's invitation be pressed upon their hearts as you draw them to Christ. And may none of them commit the unpardonable sin by hardening their hearts and becoming calloused to the conviction of your Holy Spirit. Amen."

Don Walton

Chapter 12

LET THERE BE LIGHT

The Bible teaches that unbelievers are blinded by Satan to the gospel. For instance, the Apostle Paul taught the Corinthians, *"But if our gospel be hid, it is hid to them that are lost: In whom the god of this world hath blinded the minds of them which believe not, lest the light of the glorious gospel of Christ, who is the image of God, should shine unto them"* (2 Corinthians 4:3–4). It takes more than a Christian tract or a preacher's three point sermon and poem for unbelievers to see the truth of the gospel. According to Paul, it requires God, *"who commanded the light to shine out of darkness,"* to shine His light in sinners' hearts so that they can see His glory *"in the face of Jesus Christ"* (2 Corinthians 4:6).

Your lost loved ones and friends will never see the glory of God in the face of Jesus unless God's commandment, *"Let there be light,"* is spoken in their hearts. You may persistently and proficiently proclaim the gospel to them; however, they will never see its truth through the blind eyes of their unbelief. Only God's lifting of the satanic shroud from their blinded eyes and illuminating of their darkened hearts can enable them to see the truth of the gospel.

LET THERE BE LIGHT

In Genesis 1:2, we are told that *"the earth was without form, and void; and darkness was upon the face of the deep."* The expression *"without form and void"* could be translated as *"meaningless and empty."* Before God commanded, *"Let there be light" (Genesis 1:3)*, the earth was meaningless, empty, and covered with darkness.

The earth would have remained in darkness had *"the Spirit of God"* not began moving *"upon the face of the waters."* Once the Spirit moved, *"God said, Let there be light: and there was light."* Suddenly, the light broke forth, and the earth was no longer formless and void.

Before God's commandment, *"Let there be light,"* is spoken in their hearts, unbelievers are in darkness. In darkness, the Word of God is meaningless and empty to them. They see nothing in it, so it means nothing to them.

In 2 Timothy 3:7, the Apostle Paul describes the lost as *"ever learning, and never able to come to the knowledge of the truth."* Have you ever wondered why your lost loved ones cannot grasp the truth of God's Word? According to Paul, it is because their *"understanding"* is *"darkened"* due to *"the blindness of their hearts" (Ephesians 4:18)*. As long as a veil remains over their hearts *(2 Corinthians 3:14–15)*, they will never see the truth, no matter how many times we attempt to show it to them.

Our lost family and friends are doomed to remain in darkness until the Spirit of God begins moving in their hearts. Once the Spirit moves, God gives the commandment, *"Let there be light."*

Suddenly, light breaks forth in their hearts. The Word of God is no longer meaningless and empty. It is illuminated so that its truth can be seen. Miraculously, blinded eyes are opened, beholding for the first time *"the glory of the Lord."*

U-TURNS ON DAMASCUS ROAD

The Apostle Paul taught that the gospel was not *"received"* by him from man. No man *"taught"* it to him. Instead, he received it *"by the revelation of Jesus Christ" (Galatians 1:11–12)*. Jesus Christ revealed it to him. When Christ revealed Himself to Paul on the Damascus Road, Paul made a U-turn in his life. The great persecutor of the church suddenly became the great preacher of Christ *(Acts 9:1–22)*.

It is not that Paul had never heard the message of the gospel before he ran into the divine roadblock on Damascus Road. He had heard Stephen, the first Christian martyr, boldly proclaim the message *(Acts 7:58)*. Paul's problem was that he had never seen the truth of the gospel until the light *"suddenly shined round about him"* on the road to Damascus *(Acts 9:3)*.

It took a *"revelation of Jesus Christ"* to reveal the truth of the gospel to Paul, and it will take nothing less to reveal it to our lost family and friends. Although the lost need to hear the message of the gospel from us, it takes Christ to reveal the truth of the gospel to them. The witness of our words and deeds, as well as a revelation of Christ, are both essential to the salvation of the lost. The former without the latter, however, will never turn anyone's life around.

Don Walton

TRUE CONFESSIONS

In Matthew chapter 16, Jesus asked His disciples, *"Whom do men say that I the Son of man am?"* His disciples informed Him that public opinion ranged from Elijah, come back from Heaven; to John the Baptist; to Jeremiah; or to one of the other prophets, come back from the dead. Jesus then asked, *"But whom say ye that I am?"* Simon Peter immediately answered, *"Thou art the Christ, the Son of the living God."* Jesus responded to Peter's confession by saying to him, *"Blessed art thou, Simon Barjona: for flesh and blood hath not revealed it unto thee, but my Father which is in heaven."*

Jesus' response to Peter's dramatic confession proves that no one is introduced to Christ merely through human instruction. Peter was not taught the identity of Christ by man, nor did he figure it out for himself. He received it by divine revelation when God the *"Father"* revealed it to him.

If the lost are ever to confess Christ, they must receive divine revelation. This is what Paul meant when he wrote to the Corinthians, *"No man can say that Jesus is the Lord, but by the Holy Ghost"* *(1 Corinthians 12:3)*. Although one may know *"Christ after the flesh"* with the help of human tutelage *(2 Corinthians 5:16)*, no one can confess *"Jesus is Lord"* without being enlightened and enabled by the Holy Spirit.

Why did our Lord forbid His disciples, following Peter's confession, from telling anyone *"that he was Jesus the Christ"* *(Matthew 16:20)*. Was it not because the Holy Spirit had not yet come? Without the Holy Spirit to enlighten men to the person of Christ and enable men to profess Christ, the preaching of the gospel is simply an exercise in futility. This is why Christ commanded His disciples to wait in Jerusalem for *"the promise of the Father"* (Acts 1:4). He knew His disciples' preaching of Him would be to no avail until the Spirit came. It was not until after Pentecost that Christ expected His disciples to carry out the Great Commission by telling the entire world about Him.

It is our job to tell the world about Jesus. It is the Spirit's job to enlighten men to the person of Christ and to enable them to profess Christ. If our witness to the world is to prove successful, it must be coupled with divine revelation. God the Father must reveal His Son to the lost. God does this today through the work of His Holy Spirit. Thus, both our witness and the Spirit's work are indispensable to the salvation of our lost family and friends.

PRAYER

"I praise you, Father of lights, in whom there is no darkness at all. I pray that you would speak your commandment, 'Let there be light,' into the hearts of the lost for whom I am burdened so that they may see your glory in the face of Jesus Christ. Please lift the veil from their darkened hearts so that they may come to know that Jesus is the Christ, the Son of the living God. O how I pray that the Holy Spirit will enable them to confess Jesus as Lord so that they may be saved! Amen."

Don Walton

Chapter 13

LIFTING UP JESUS

I n John 3:14–15, Jesus said, *"And as Moses lifted up the serpent in the wilderness, even so must the Son of man be lifted up: That whosoever believeth in him should not perish, but have eternal life."* The similarities between Moses lifting up the brazen serpent in the wilderness and Christ being lifted up on the cross of Calvary prove that the brazen serpent serves as an Old Testament type of Christ. Let's consider the parallels between the two.

THE BRAZEN SERPENT

First, consider the parallel between Israel's problem in Moses' day and mankind's problem today. The Israelites had been bitten by venomous serpents *(Numbers 21:4–6)*. These poisonous serpent bites were proving fatal. Like the ancient Israelites, we, too, have been snake bitten. All of mankind was bitten by the serpent in the Garden of Eden when Adam and Eve succumbed to temptation. Sin—the serpent's fatal bite—has afflicted all men ever since Adam because *"all have sinned" (Romans 5:12)*.

Second, consider the parallel between Israel's desperate situation and ours. Israel was in desperate need of a cure because without it they would die. How much more desperate is our predicament? Without a remedy for sin, we, too will perish not just physically but spiritually as well.

Finally, consider the parallels between Israel's healing in Moses' day and our salvation today: (1) Israel's cure, like ours, was shaped into the likeness of that which wounded. The cure for Israel's serpent bites was bronze fashioned into the form of a serpent *(Numbers 21:7–9)*. The cure for our sin is Jesus Christ who came into this world in the form of a man and became man's sin on the cross of Calvary *(Philippians 2:7–8; 2 Corinthians 5:21)*. (2) The brazen serpent had no poison but was fashioned into the form of a venomous snake. Likewise, Christ had no sin, but He became sin on our behalf. (3) To effect a cure the brazen serpent had to be lifted up on a pole. All who looked to it in faith were saved. To effect our salvation, Jesus Christ had to be lifted up on a cross, and all who look to Him in faith are saved.

WE WOULD SEE JESUS

In John 12:20–22, some Greeks entreated Philip, *"Sir, we would see Jesus."* Philip, being unaccustomed to such an unusual request—to see Jesus rather than receive something from Him—went and told Andrew. Together, Andrew and Philip reported the Greeks' unusual request to Jesus.

Hearing of the Greeks' desire to see Him, Jesus responded by speaking of His impending death *(John 12:23–27)*. He then added, to signify the kind of death He would die, *"And I, if I be lifted up from the earth, will draw all men unto me"* *(John 12: 32–33)*. By such a strange response to the Greeks' request, Jesus appears to be teaching us that the only place to truly see Him is on the cross.

THE PAINTING

A man once traveled to a small village in Europe. Before his departure, a friend, who had visited the same village a couple of years earlier, insisted that he take the time to visit the village chapel and see its painting. On his flight to Europe, a fellow passenger, learning of the man's destination, also implored him to see the chapel's painting while in the small village. Upon his arrival at the village inn, the innkeeper urged him to visit the chapel and see its painting during his stay.

Overcome by curiosity, the man quickly unpacked his bags and took off in search of the village chapel. Finding the chapel, he discovered the front door was locked. He knocked, but there was no answer. As he turned to leave, the door creaked opened. The chapel's caretaker peeked out and acutely observed, "You've come to see the painting?" When the man nodded, the elderly caretaker invited him in.

Once inside, the caretaker led the man to a dimly lit hallway in the back of the building. On the wall at the opposite end of the hall was a painting of Christ hanging on the cross. The painting, however, appeared grossly distorted and out of proportion.

The man immediately reacted, "I don't understand. Why all the fuss over this painting?" In reply, the caretaker instructed him to get down a little and to come a little closer. The man promptly bent down and walked a couple of steps closer to the painting.

Still, it made no sense to him. Again and again, the caretaker entreated, "Get down and come closer." Again and again, the man complied until he finally fell on his knees at the foot of the painting. Looking up, it suddenly made sense to him. Everything was in proper proportion. The artist, it turns out, had painted the painting from the perspective of someone kneeling at the cross.

Our lost friends and family will never truly see Jesus until they kneel at the cross. Only then will it all make sense to them. Therefore, we should pray for them to see Christ crucified. Once they do, Christ will be able to draw them unto Himself.

JESUS CHRIST AND HIM CRUCIFIED

In Galatians 3:1, the Apostle Paul asked the Christians in Galatia the following question: *"O foolish Galatians, who hath bewitched you, that ye should not obey the truth, before whose eyes Jesus Christ hath been evidently set forth, crucified among you?"* Paul's preaching in Galatia had clearly portrayed to the Galatians the crucified Christ. It was, therefore, inconceivable to Paul that those *"before whose eyes Jesus Christ had been evidently set forth crucified"* could be so easily *"bewitched"* by others.

That the aim of Paul's preaching was to portray the crucified Christ to others is evident from the apostle's own words in 1 Corinthians 1:23 and 2:1–5, where Paul claims to preach nothing *"save Jesus Christ, and him crucified."* Paul understood that the preaching of the cross alone lifted up Jesus so that He could draw all men unto Himself. Thus, Paul used his preaching to paint word pictures of Christ on the cross. As a result, those who heard Paul saw the crucified Christ and were drawn into the arms of God's unconditional love.

Have you ever heard an old-timer pray for God to hide your preacher behind the cross? Although such prayers were frequently heard in days gone by, they are becoming increasingly rare in our churches today. The need, however, of people's attention being focused on what Christ did for them on the cross instead of on how well the preacher is doing in the pulpit is every bit as important today as it was yesterday.

Too often churchgoers leave church talking about how good their preacher is but not about how wonderful their Savior is. Such focus upon the men in the pulpit, rather than upon the man on the cross, is proof of the failure of modern-day preaching. When men are praising preachers and being drawn to them instead of praising Christ and being drawn to Him, something is horribly wrong in the pulpits of our day.

The Apostle Paul said that his preaching was *"in weakness, and in fear, and in much trembling"* without *"excellency of speech or enticing words of man's wisdom."* Some who heard Paul preach called *"his bodily presence weak, and his speech contemptible" (2 Corinthians 10:10)*. Still, Paul was unmoved by such assessments of himself. He understood that the purpose of preaching was to proclaim Christ and not to promote oneself *(2 Corinthians 4:5)*.

Although Paul's preaching never resulted in men being impressed with him, it did result in men praising God because of him *(Galatians 1:23–24)*. Paul would have had it no other way. Anytime attention began to be diverted from Christ to himself,

Paul dodged it by quickly ducking behind the cross *(1 Corinthians 3:4–7)*. His insistence upon his own insignificance and upon Christ's supremacy made for successful preaching.

The purpose of preaching is to lift up Jesus so that men can see what He has done for them on the cross. Only when they see Christ on the cross will men be drawn to Him. If the preacher fails at this, he has failed. It doesn't matter how eloquent his speech is or how spellbinding his oratory. It's not even important how many brag on his sermons. If his preaching doesn't result in others boasting in the cross, all is lost!

LIFTING UP JESUS

What is our lost and dying world's greatest need? Is it not the Gospel of Jesus Christ? What all men need most is to hear what Christ has done for them on the cross. Until they do, there is no hope of their coming to Christ.

When Jonas Salk developed his famous polio vaccine, a friend advised him to wait a while before offering it to the world. According to Salk's friend, waiting would result in a far more lucrative deal for Salk. Salk immediately rejected his friend's advice, insisting that he who has what the world needs is a debtor to the whole world.

As one entrusted with the Gospel of Jesus Christ, the Apostle Paul saw himself as a *"debtor both to the Greeks, and to the Barbarians; both to the wise, and to the unwise" (Romans 1:14)*. Possessing what the whole world needed, namely the Gospel of Jesus Christ, Paul saw himself as a *"debtor"* to the entire world.

This is why he was always *"ready to preach the gospel"* to anyone, at anytime, anywhere *(Romans 1:15)*. Paul felt he owed it to everyone.

As the sole steward of the Gospel of Jesus Christ, the church owes the world its witness. If we don't lift up Jesus so that our lost and dying world can see what He has done for them on the cross, who will? It is up to us to share with the lost what they desperately need and what we alone possess. If we fail to lift up Jesus by preaching the gospel, the lost will never be drawn to Him.

This explains the Apostle Paul's bold declaration in Romans 1:16: *"For I am not ashamed of the gospel of Christ: for it is the power of God unto salvation to every one that believeth; to the Jew first, and also to the Greek."* As far as Paul was concerned, the cross was the church's big draw. He was proud to proclaim it, realizing that its proclamation resulted in *"the power of God unto salvation to every one that believeth."*

Unfortunately, much of today's church appears ashamed of the gospel. How else can we explain our mimicking of Hollywood in looking for the hottest names and most famous stars to attract our crowds and secure the success of our undertakings? It is as though we have lost all confidence in the drawing power of the cross. Unlike Paul, who saw the cross as the church's biggest draw, much of today's church feels the cross is not enough. Thus, we turn to celebrity testimonies, well-known preachers, best-selling authors, famous recording artists, contemporary services, multimedia, and mass marketing to draw our audiences and fill our auditoriums.

As if this sorry state of affairs were not bad enough, there is an ever-increasing segment in today's church that sees the cross as an obstacle to drawing people instead of as the object for drawing them. Thanks to this growing constituency, the cross is often kept hidden from view, at least, until we feel it's safe to drag it out. God forbid that we should boldly preach the cross as the only hope for lost, immortal souls. Such preaching is condemned by proponents of the soft sell as negative and counterproductive in reaching the sensitive, broadminded, and politically-correct lost souls of our day. In lieu of the unapologetic preaching of the gospel, much of today's church is opting to lure the lost in with a myriad of religious trinkets. Once the lost have been baited with the trinkets of our church or denomination, the gospel can then be carefully slipped in, hopefully, in such a subtle way as not to offend anyone.

All over Christendom, Christians are boldly proclaiming what their church or denomination is doing. They are busy lifting up their church's pastor, programs, ministries, and facilities. Few, however, are preaching the cross and lifting up Christ. Consequently, many people are coming to church, especially to those churches with more programs, better-known preachers, and bigger facilities, but few people are coming to Christ.

Make no mistake about it. Our lost loved ones and friends will never come to Christ unless someone lifts Him up to them! They don't need to hear what a pastor, church, or denomination can do for them. They need to hear what Jesus has done for them on the cross. They don't need to see famous celebrities, televangelists, or Hollywood-like extravaganzas. They need to see Jesus Christ and

Him crucified. Until they see the crucified Christ, there is no hope for their salvation.

We must pray that God will use us or one of our fellow believers to lift up Jesus to our lost friends and family. Once Jesus is lifted up to them, He can draw them unto Himself. Until then, there is no hope of their kneeling at the cross and beholding for themselves the crucified Christ.

PRAYER

"I praise you, O God, for you are high and lifted up. I thank you for lifting up your Son on Calvary's cross so that all who believe in Him shall not perish but have eternal life. I pray that you will use me or a fellow believer to lift up Jesus to the lost for whom I am burdened so that they may be drawn to Him. Furthermore, as a steward of the gospel and as a debtor to the entire world, I pray that you will make me ever-ready to boldly proclaim the gospel message to others so that they may kneel at the foot of the cross and behold for themselves the crucified Christ! Amen."

Don Walton

Chapter 14
PRAYING FOR PRODIGALS

The fifteenth chapter of the Gospel of Luke is about lost things. Jesus spoke about a lost sheep (verses 3–7), a lost coin (verses 8–10), and a lost boy (verses 11–24). In using these three parables to make a single point, Jesus emphasized the importance of the lost to God. What matters to God is that the lost are found. Why else would God have sent his Son into the world *"to seek and to save that which was lost" (Luke 19:10)*?

Along with stressing the importance of the lost to God, Jesus' three parables in Luke chapter fifteen also teach us that all lost people are not the same. Some are like lost sheep, others are like lost coins, and some are like the prodigal son.

THE LOST SHEEP

Sheep get lost because of their own carelessness. They get their eyes on a clump of grass here and a clump of grass there. Before long, they've wandered off from the flock and gotten lost.

Some lost people are like lost sheep. They are lost because of their own carelessness. They've been careless all of their lives about the things of God. They've had their eyes on a clump of worldly pleasure here and a clump of worldly possessions there.

Their obsession with worldly things has led to their carelessness in spiritual things.

THE LOST COIN

Unlike the lost sheep, the lost coin was not lost because of its own carelessness. Instead, it was lost because of the carelessness of another. The woman would not have lost one of her ten pieces of silver had she not gotten careless with it.

Some lost people are like the lost coin. They are lost because of someone else's carelessness. Some are lost because of the carelessness of parents who failed to *"bring them up in the nurture and admonition of the Lord" (Ephesians 6:4)*. Others are lost because of the carelessness of Christian friends who fail to pray for them and witness to them. Still, some are lost because of the carelessness of a nearby church in reaching out to its community.

THE LOST BOY

When we come to the prodigal son, we are no longer discussing lost sheep or lost coins. We are not talking about the careless but the calloused. Prodigals are the hard-core lost souls of our world. They are those who live their lives with a clinched fist in the face of God.

THE PARABLE OF THE PRODIGAL SON

Jesus Christ was the Master Teacher. His favorite method of teaching was the parable. Parables are earthly stories with heavenly meanings. Of all our Lord's parables, His most famous is the parable of the prodigal son *(Luke 15:11–24)*.

The prodigal son wished to leave his father's house because he no longer wanted to live under his father's rule. Therefore, he demanded his portion of the inheritance. By making such a demand prior to his father's death, the prodigal was disowning his own. As far as he was concerned, he would live the rest of his life as though his father were dead.

The prodigal in this parable represents the lost. The father represents God. Our world is full of lost people who demand an inheritance from God. They believe God owes them health, prosperity, and happiness. At the same time, however, they insist upon living their lives as though God were dead. They live each day as they please without any thought of pleasing God. Essentially, they live as if God didn't exist.

After receiving his inheritance from his father's gracious hand, the prodigal left his father's house and *"took his journey into a far country."* There, he *"wasted his substance with riotous living."* The *"far country"* in this parable represents the world. Prodigal souls are glad to receive divine benevolence from God's gracious hand. They do so without feeling even slightly beholden to their Heavenly Benefactor. This explains how they can live riotously in this world, unconscionably squandering all with which God has blessed them.

At first, the Prodigal son was having the time of his life in the far country. His life was filled with friends and frolicking as long as his pockets were filled with his father's money. There is, as the

Bible teaches, pleasure in sin for a season *(Hebrews 11:25)*. The trouble is sin's season is short-lived. One scarcely begins to enjoy sin's pleasures when the harsh reality of its cold winter sets in. Sin's fleeting pleasures quickly give way to its cruel and inevitable consequences, so what begins as a momentary pleasure ends up with a lifetime price tag.

The world is a false friend. The prodigal son, like countless others, learned this lesson the hard way. He had plenty of buddies as long as he was buying their drinks at the corner bar. Several pretty girls competed for his company as long as he was pulling cash from his pockets, but the moment he pulled out lint instead of lucre, he suddenly found himself without a friend in sight.

The world always taps for its friends those who are willing to pick up its tab. As long as a person proves useful to the world's ends, he is in no danger of being thrown to the wind. The moment that person outlives his usefulness, however, is the moment the world will throw him away like last week's magazine.

Penniless and friendless, the prodigal son soon found himself in dire straits when *"a mighty famine"* arose in the land. Forced by famine into panhandling for survival, the prodigal quickly discovered the pitilessness of the far country. Despite his begging, *"no man gave unto him,"* not even his former female companions or barroom buddies. As a last resort, the prodigal accepted employment from *"a citizen of that country"* who *"sent him into the fields to feed swine."* Nothing could have been more demoralizing or less kosher to this young Jewish upstart than this.

There is always a famine in the far country, that is, in the world. Nothing in this fallen world can satisfy the famished soul.

Try as he may, nothing in this world will ever fill the void in the sinner's heart or the emptiness of his life. God and God alone can satisfy the hungry soul *(Psalm 107:9)*. No one else can help, no matter how much the sinner begs.

In the parable of the prodigal son, the *"citizen of that country"* represents the devil, the prince and god of this world *(John 12:31; 2 Corinthians 4:4)*. Eventually, every prodigal son ends up in the devil's pigpen. Forced to turn to Satan, due to their famished souls, prodigals are swiftly reduced to living with spiritual swine.

SPIRITUAL SWINE

In Mark 5:1–20, Jesus cast a *"Legion"* of demons out of the demoniac of Gadara into a *"herd of swine."* Afterward, the swine ran off a cliff into the sea, preferring their own destruction to demonic possession. Why would Jesus do such a cruel thing to swine? Granted, pigs are not the most domesticated of God's creatures but creatures of God, nonetheless.

In the Old Testament, God prohibited the Israelites from eating pork *(Leviticus 11:1–8)*. He also forbade them from having any contact with a pig's carcass. In Colossians 2:15–17, the Apostle Paul teaches, among other things, that the unclean creatures of the Old Testament were physical types of spiritual truths in the New Testament. What unclean animals such as swine were to Israel in the physical realm, unclean spirits—the *"principalities and powers"* that Christ *"triumphed over"* on the cross—are to the church in the spiritual realm.

Demons are called *"unclean spirits"* twenty-five times in the New Testament. The word *"unclean"* is also used in Acts 10:11–14 to refer to certain animals that the Israelites were forbidden to eat. One of these unclean animals was the pig. Just as Israel was to zealously guard itself from all contact with physical swine, Christians are to guard themselves zealously from all contact with spiritual swine—demons. This is why the Apostle Paul in 1 Corinthians 10:20–21 commands Christians to have no *"fellowship with demons."*

Gadara, the home of the demoniac delivered by Jesus in Mark 5:1–20, was the land given to the tribe of Gad on the east side of the Jordan River. Remember, the tribe of Gad along with the tribe of Reuben and half the tribe of Manasseh chose to remain on the wrong side of the Jordan *(Numbers 32:1–42)*. By the time Christ came, the Gadarenes were so degenerate that they had gone into the pig business. Far from living up to God's Law, the Gadarenes were making a living breaking it.

By casting demons out of the demoniac into the swine, Jesus was showing the Gadarenes the only solution to the swine problem. The people of God must not live with swine but must rid themselves of them. In spite of such a powerful object lesson, the people of Gadara requested Christ's departure from their coasts. In the end, they preferred living with swine to the Savior's living in their midst.

All who live in rebellion against God, whether they be prodigal sons or Gadarenes, end up living with swine. To one degree or another, all pig feeders and farmers end up demonized. This is not to say that all lost people are demon possessed. It is to say, however, that all lost people are demonized. Our lost friends and family may not be possessed like the demoniac of Gadara. They may be merely oppressed like the prodigal or obsessed like the Gadarenes. Still, consciously or unconsciously, their lives are being unduly swayed by spiritual swine.

Rock Bottom

According to Jesus, the prodigal son sank so low and became so desperate that he considered eating *"the husks that the swine did eat."* For someone like myself who has slopped hogs, it's hard to imagine somebody sinking low enough to eat hog slop. Yet, sin's degradation is fathomless. Many a prodigal son has pulled up a chair at *"the table of devils"* to feast on their husks *(1 Corinthians 10:21)*.

It was at this point when he hit rock bottom that the prodigal son finally *"came to himself."* The implication is clear: until he came to himself, the prodigal son must have been beside himself. What other explanation is there, apart from insanity, for leaving the father's house to live in the far country? Truly, all who live in rebellion against a loving Heavenly Father are beside themselves.

Once he came to his senses, the prodigal son asked himself, "What am I doing here?" It dawned on him that he did not have to stay with the swine and starve. He could return home to his father's house and ask his father to *"make him one of his hired servants."* He understood that he was *"no longer worthy to be called* [his father's] *son."* Still, he hoped his father could find it within his heart to forgive him and hire him as a servant. As his father's servant, he would at least have plenty to eat and not *"perish with hunger."*

THE FATHER'S HOUSE

How many times do you suppose the prodigal son rehearsed his apology to his father on the long trip home from the far country? After countless rehearsals and seemingly endless miles, the prodigal finally caught sight of the old home place. From a far distance, he could make out the familiar contours of the father's house. Little did he know, however, that he, too, had been spotted by a far away watchful eye.

Jesus said that *"the father saw"* the prodigal son while he *"was yet a great way off."* Why do you suppose the Father spotted the prodigal the moment he came back into view from the far country? Could it be that the father had been on a daily vigil ever since his son left home? Since the day the prodigal departed, the father had been standing at the front window, looking down the road, and hoping his wayward son would soon be seen making his way back home.

As the prodigal neared the house, his father came running down the road to meet him. I can't help but wonder what the prodigal thought when he saw his dad running in his direction. Perhaps, he expected to hear the father say, "How dare you come back here. You get out of here, and don't ever come back. You're no longer welcome in this house." Maybe, he feared something even worse like receiving from his father the beating of his life. He had, after all, disowned his father and disgraced the family name.

Imagine the prodigal's surprise when the father *"fell on his neck and kissed him."* Far from running him off or beating him down, the father welcomed him home with open arms. The father's kiss was proof that the prodigal was still loved and that in spite of the prodigal's sins against the father the father's love for the prodigal remained unchanged.

In Romans 8:35–39, the Apostle Paul teaches us that nothing can separate us from the love of God. There is absolutely nothing that can change the way God feels about us. His love for us is unconditional and unchanging. This explains how Jesus could promise to receive all who come to Him *(John 6:37)*. Every prodigal soul who comes home from the far country will be greeted with a kiss by the Heavenly Father.

Not only was the prodigal son still loved, he was still in the family. This is proven by the father's instructing of his servants to put *"shoes"* on the prodigal son's feet. Only servants went barefoot. All family members wore shoes. The prodigal was a son not a servant. He would never live in the bunkhouse but would always reside in his father's house.

Along with putting shoes on the prodigal's feet, the father also instructed his servants to put a ring on the prodigal's hand. This ring was a sign of heirship, proving to all who saw it that the prodigal son was still his father's heir. Everything the father possessed was promised to the prodigal.

Whenever prodigal souls turn from the far country to faith in Christ, they receive from Christ the *"power to become the sons of God" (John 1:12)*. Christians are not simply servants of God. We are much more; we are the children of God. We have been born by God's Spirit into God's family through faith in God's Son. Having *"received the Spirit of adoption,"* we alone can cry out to God, *"Abba, Father" (Romans 8:15)*.

The word *"Abba,"* used by the Apostle Paul in Romans 8:15, is an interesting word. It is an Aramaic word equivalent to our English word *daddy*. According to Jewish tradition, servants were forbidden from addressing the head of the family by this title. The only ones permitted to use this title when addressing the head of the family were his children.

In Ephesians 3:14–15, the Apostle Paul identifies *"the Father of our Lord Jesus Christ"* as the one *"of whom the whole family in heaven and earth is named."* God the Father is the Head of the family. Therefore, no servant has the right to cry out to God, *"Abba, Father."* It is only the children of God who can call Him "Daddy."

Not only are Christians children of God, we are also heirs of God. The Bible teaches us that we are *"heirs of God, and joint-heirs with Christ" (Romans 8:17)*. All of God's possessions are promised to believers in Christ. Truly, our Heavenly Father has put a ring on our finger and shoes on our feet. He has adopted us into His family and promised us His possessions.

In addition to shoes and a ring, the prodigal son's homecoming netted him a new outfit. His father commanded the servants to *"bring forth the best robe and put it on him."* Undoubtedly, the prodigal son had returned home in rags ruined by the stain of sin and reeking with the stench of swine. For this reason, the father insisted that his repentant son's unseemly apparel be replaced with the most comely of garments.

Anytime a prodigal soul returns home to the Heavenly Father's house, he is forced to do so in the filthy rags of his own righteousness *(Isaiah 64:6)*. Our righteousness is made filthy by the stain of sin. No matter how hard we try to do right, we always come short of what God requires *(Romans 3:23)*. Only one person has ever lived up to God's requirements—the Lord Jesus Christ. Thanks to His sinless life and substitutionary death, prodigals can come home to the Father's house. When we do, our sinful rags are exchanged for the seamless robe of Christ's perfect righteousness *(Isaiah 61:10; John 19:23–24)*.

So overjoyed was the father at the prodigal's homecoming that he ordered his servants *"to bring the fatted calf, and kill it."* He wanted everyone to *"eat and be merry."* It was a time for unparalleled celebration. The father's son *"was dead"* but now was *"alive again."* He had been *"lost,"* but now he was *"found."*

It seems most ironic that after leaving his father's house to party in the far country the prodigal son returned home to have the party of all parties thrown in his honor. Everything the prodigal had ever wanted was right there in his father's house all along. Just think of the trouble he could have saved himself if he had only known this before he went traipsing off into the far country.

According to Jesus, there is a party thrown in our Heavenly Father's house every time a sinner repents *(Luke 15:7, 10)*. In fact, Heaven parties more hardily *"over one sinner that repents"* than it does *"over ninety nine just persons, which need no repentance."* Just think about it. Every time a lost person is saved, Heaven throws a party in his honor.

Christians can rest assured that they were once the source of Heaven's greatest joy. "When was that?" we may ask. It was on the day of their salvation. On that day, our Heavenly Father commanded all of Heaven to *"be merry,"* because each of us, His long *"lost"* child, had at last been *"found!"*

Praying For Prodigals

Although our Heavenly Father has already thrown a party in our honor on the day of our salvation, we can still help Heaven throw parties by praying for prodigals. When it comes to praying for prodigals, no prayer we ever pray will require more courage. Make no mistake about it, praying for these hard-core lost souls of our world is not a task for the weak-kneed. Only the most daring among us will ever effectively kneel in prayer for the salvation of prodigal souls.

Remember, we are talking about prodigal sons and not lost sheep or coins. We are not talking about carelessness but callousness. Prodigals are not lost because of their carelessness; they are lost because of their callousness. They live their lives with a clinched fist in the face of the Almighty. They have, as the Apostle Paul wrote, *"no fear of God before their eyes" (Romans 3:18)*. They neither revere God nor regard Him.

In such hard cases, what hope is there of salvation? As we have already learned, there is no hope of salvation for anyone apart from a miracle of God. Thus, the salvation of prodigal souls requires nothing different in this regard than the salvation of others. The difference is found in the drastic measures required for prodigals to come to themselves. Don't forget, the prodigal son had to go to the pigpen before *"he came to himself."* Only after hitting rock bottom did he finally decide to turn from his sin and return to his father.

Too often today, Christians are guilty of keeping prodigals out of the pigpen. For instance, how many Christian parents are in the habit of bailing their rebellious children out of all their troubles? By shielding their children from the consequences of their actions, these misguided parents effectively remove from their obstinate offspring any incentive to ever mend their ways.

Even today's church has gotten into the business of keeping prodigals out of the pigpen. Much of what passes for social ministry in our churches is really nothing more than a safety net for high flying sinners. Thanks to our social ministries, many daring sinners continue their high wire act without any fear of falling. Why should they fear falling from sin's dangerous heights as long as the church is there to catch them with homeless shelters, food pantries, and clothes closets?

Now, I'm not against homeless shelters, food pantries, and clothes closets, but these ministries should be used to provide for the poor and not to provide prodigals with protection from the pigpen. The ultimate purpose of all church ministries should be to reach people for Jesus Christ. Social ministries can be an effective way of reaching the needy. Christ taught us this Himself by frequently reaching others by ministering first to their physical needs.

Though very effective in reaching the poor, social ministries can also be counter-productive in reaching prodigals. Many prodigals never find themselves *"in want"* despite the fact that they *"waste* [their] *substance with riotous living."* They are never forced to choose between the pigpen and the father's house. Thanks to the church's willingness to feed, house, and clothe them, they can

113

continue living in disobedience to God without any fear of suffering destitution. Aided and abetted by the church, these prodigals have no incentive to ever come to their senses.

Instead of keeping them out of the pigpen, we should be praying prodigals into it. That's right! We should pray for them to hit rock bottom. Prodigals will never consider turning to Christ until sin's consequences catch up to them. It normally entails the collapse of the prodigal's whole world to bring him to his senses. Thus, we should pray for his world to collapse. We should never lend him a hand in keeping it patched together.

Before you accuse me of being hardhearted, let me remind you that the father in the parable of the prodigal son never intervened on his son's behalf. He permitted his son to leave home, even though he knew the boy was destined for the pigpen. Furthermore, he never attempted in any way to catch his son before he hit rock bottom. Not once did he send a servant to the far country to check on the boy. The father simply let him go and let him alone.

Sometimes, the best way to help those we love is by not helping them at all. Any help we offer will only prevent them from learning their lesson, and apart from learning their lesson, there is no hope of their life being changed. To stand by while friends and family make their way to the pigpen is difficult. To pray for the acceleration of the process is even harder. Still, the practice of such tough-love is essential for the salvation of prodigal souls.

PRAYER

"I praise you, my Heavenly Father, for welcoming a sinner like me into your family with open arms. I thank you for your indescribable gifts of

grace: a kiss for my cheek, a robe for my back, a ring for my finger, and shoes for my feet. I cry out to you, 'Abba, Father'; asking that I might bring you as much joy today as I did on the day of my salvation!

I pray now on behalf of the prodigal souls for whom I am burdened. I ask you to bring them to their senses, no matter what it takes, so that they will come to Christ in confession of their sins against Heaven. Please, bring them to themselves so that they will repent and all of Heaven rejoice. Amen."

Don Walton

Chapter 15
PRAYING DOWN STRONGHOLDS

In Luke 11:14–20, Jesus cast a demon out of a dumb person. Afterward, the mute spoke and all the people marveled. To counter the wonderment of the people, the religious leaders accused Jesus of *"casting out devils through Beelzebub the chief of devils."* Dismissing their accusation as ludicrous because no kingdom divides itself against itself, Jesus pointed out to the religious leaders that His casting out demons *"with the finger of God"* proved that *"the kingdom of God"* had come upon them.

Jesus continues to speak about the demonic in Luke 11: 21–22 when He compares demons to heavily armed strongmen. According to Jesus, demonic powers will never give up their *"palaces"* and *"goods"* until someone stronger comes along, stripping them of their *"armor."* Only then can the goods of strongmen be taken and the spoils divided.

Jesus Christ is stronger than demons *(1 John 4:4)*. He came into this world to strip devils of their armor and to spoil their goods. This is why the Apostle John writes, *"For this purpose the Son of God was manifested, that he might destroy the works of the devil" (1 John 3:8)*. Christ's whole ministry consisted of displacing, defeating, and dispossessing the devil.

As Christ's church, we are commissioned by Him to continue His ministry in this world. Like our Lord, we are to strip strongmen of their armor and spoil their goods. Nowhere is this more important than in the church's snatching of men's immortal souls from Satan's clutches.

BINDING THE STRONGMAN

In Matthew 12:29, Jesus asked, *"How can one enter into a strong man's house, and spoil his goods, except he first bind the strong man?"* Satan is the *"strong man"* and lost souls are his *"goods."* Before Satan's goods can be spoiled, that is, before the lost can be saved, the *"strong man"* must be bound, but how do we bind the *"strong man"*?

In 2 Corinthians 10:3–6, the Apostle Paul teaches the necessity of spiritual warfare and the futility of carnal weapons in bringing men *"to obedience to Christ."* This teaching of the apostle should once and for all dismiss the naive notion in today's church that all it takes to reach the lost for Christ is a good outreach program. The salvation of lost souls requires nothing less than spiritual war. Make no mistake about it, prayer is warfare, especially when praying for the lost.

Samuel Chadwick once said, "He [the devil] laughs at our toil, mocks at our wisdom, but trembles when we pray." The saints bowing their heads and bending their knees on behalf of sinners is no laughing matter to Satan. Thus, prayer warriors volunteering for front-line service should expect the fiercest fighting of all. Satan is not about to sit idly by while we drop to our knees in a strategic offensive designed to bind him and spoil his goods. Instead, he will counterattack with a ferociousness that only prayerful importunity can prevail against.

According to the Apostle Paul, Satan will not be bound in men's lives so that they can come *"to obedience to Christ"* until *"strongholds,"* *"imaginations,"* and every other *"high thing that exalts itself against the knowledge of God"* is pulled down and demolished. Carnal weapons, such as manmade church programs, are totally inadequate when it comes to the *"pulling down of strongholds."* Only spiritual weapons, which are *"mighty through God,"* are sufficient for pulling down strongholds, binding the strongman, and seizing spiritual spoils.

STRONGHOLDS

What is a stronghold? In the Bible, strongholds were fortresses erected for protection and defense. Spiritual strongholds, like the ones referred to by the Apostle Paul in 2 Corinthians 10:4, are demonic fortresses erected in the lives of people. Their purpose is to provide protection and defense to the enemy. Hidden in their strongholds, Satan and his demons are able to keep themselves securely entrenched in people's lives.

I believe the strongman's *"armor,"* alluded to by Jesus in Luke 11:22, is synonymous with the *"strongholds"* mentioned by Paul in 2 Corinthians 10:4. Both refer to the protection and defense of the enemy. Whatever the enemy uses to keep himself securely entrenched in people's lives is his armor or stronghold. As long as Satan is suited in armor and sheltered in strongholds, there is no hope of spoiling his goods.

In Ephesians 4:27, Paul issues this solemn warning: *"Don't give place to the devil."* The Apostle Paul understood that Satan's strongholds begin with simple footholds. All the enemy initially requires is a little room to begin his operations. Soon thereafter, that little bit of elbow room quickly turns into a hostile takeover of a person's life. Before that person realizes it, Satan has erected a stronghold and suited up in his armor. Afterward, one's only hope of deliverance is divine intervention.

JERICHO

The Apostle Paul taught that the Old Testament provides us with physical illustrations of spiritual truths taught in the New Testament *(1 Corinthians 10:6)*. The New Testament teaching concerning spiritual strongholds is illustrated in the Old Testament story of the fall of Jericho *(Joshua 5:13–6:27)*.

Jericho was an enemy stronghold. It stood between the people of God and His will for their lives. For this reason, it had to be overcome, yet it was humanly impossible to overcome Jericho. Its walls could not be dug under, tunneled through, or climbed over. Therefore, Israel's only hope of victory was divine intervention. Only God could bring down the walls of Jericho; so all Israel could do was follow their God-given battle plan.

Some of our lost loved ones and friends have a spiritual Jericho in their lives. This stronghold of the enemy is keeping them from knowing God. For this reason, it must be overcome, yet overcoming it is humanly impossible. Therefore, our lost loved ones and friends have no hope of salvation apart from God's miraculous intervention. Only God can pull down Satan's strongholds in their lives; so all we can do is follow the biblical battle plan.

BINDING AND LOOSING

What is the biblical battle plan for pulling down strongholds and binding the strongman? In Matthew 16:13–19 and 18:18–20, Jesus teaches us about binding and loosing. It is in these two powerful passages that we find the secret to binding the strongman and pulling down his strongholds.

According to Roman Catholicism, the *"keys of the kingdom of heaven"* were given by Jesus to Peter alone *(Matthew 16:19)*. Thus, only Peter and his papal successors have the ability to *"bind on earth"* what is *"bound in heaven"* and to *"loose on earth"* what is *"loosed in heaven."* Though used by the Roman Catholic Church as a prop for its papacy, this erroneous teaching is a gross misinterpretation of Scripture.

The power to bind and loose was not given exclusively to Peter. It was given to all of Christ's disciples *(Matthew 18:19)*. Likewise, the *"keys of the kingdom of heaven"* are not the private possession of popes. Instead, they belong to everyone, like Peter, who knows and confesses Jesus Christ as *"the Son of the living God"* (Matthew 16:13–18).

THE KEYS TO THE KINGDOM OF HEAVEN

What are *"the keys to the kingdom of heaven"*? They are nothing more than the Christian's confession of Christ. What hope is there of Heaven being unlocked and opened to our lost and dying world apart from our profession and preaching of Christ?

As the sole steward of the gospel and the lone confessor of Christ, the church alone holds *"the keys to the kingdom of heaven."*

If we are unfaithful in our stewardship of the gospel, that is, if we fail to confess Christ to others, we will be like the Pharisees that Jesus condemned for *"shutting up the kingdom of heaven against men" (Matthew 23:13)*. In effect, we will be binding the lost over to destruction. Conversely, if we are faithful stewards of the gospel message, the kingdom of Heaven will be unlocked and opened to our lost and dying world. Men will be loosed from sin and Satan's clutches as we introduce them to Christ.

COVENANT PRAYER

Throughout the years, many have attempted to rob Jesus' words on binding and loosing of their power. They have done so by paraphrasing them: *"Whatsoever ye shall bind on earth shall be bound* [already] *in heaven: and whatsoever ye shall loose on earth shall be loosed* [already] *in heaven."* Although I agree with the gist of this, I disagree with reducing Jesus' words to mean nothing more than this.

It should go without saying that we can no more step outside of God's will or strip sovereignty from His hand in the area of binding and loosing than we can in any other area. To step out from under the authority of Heaven by attempting to do anything Christ has not commanded or commissioned is to doom our best efforts to futility. Hence, it is true, at least in this regard, that we can only bind and loose on earth what is already bound and loosed in Heaven. Still, restricting the church's binding and loosing to this alone robs Christ's promise of its power.

Does the church really have the authority to bind and loose, and if so, does this include binding the strongman and loosing the lost from his clutches? I believe the promise of Christ proves that we possess this power. The only problem is that few in today's church know how to wield it on behalf of the lost.

According to Jesus' words in Matthew 18:18–20, the church exercises this extraordinary power through covenant prayer. After promising His disciples the power to bind and loose in verse 18, Jesus said, *"Again I say unto you, That if two of you shall agree on earth as touching any thing that they shall ask, it shall be done for them of my Father which is in heaven."* Notice, Jesus begins verse 19 with the word *"again."* The word *"again"* means *"once more."* Thus, verse 19 is simply restating verse 18. It, too, promises us the power to bind and loose. The only difference is that verse 19 provides along with verse 20 the insight into how it's done.

Whenever *"two or three"* believers *"gather together in* [Christ's] *name,"* Christ promises to be *"in the midst of them."* If they have gathered together to pray for the lost, Christ, Who is *"in the midst of them,"* will reveal to them satanic strongholds. When strongholds are revealed, *"two"* or more believers can proceed to pull them down by agreeing together in prayer. Once the strongholds are pulled down, the strongman is bound, and the lost are loosed.

Confirmation by two or more witnesses has strong scriptural precedent *(Numbers 35:30; Deuteronomy 17:6, 19:15; Matthew 18:16; John 5:31–47; 2 Corinthians 13:1; 1 Timothy 5:19; Hebrews*

10:28; and 1 John 5:6–13). In light of this, we should not be surprised that the church's binding and loosing is contingent upon the agreement of at least *"two"* of us. Until Christ confirms to *"two"* or more the satanic strongholds needing to be prayed down in the lives of the lost, the strongman cannot be bound or his goods spoiled. However, once confirmed in two agreeing hearts covenanting together in prayer, the devil's strongholds can be demolished and the lost delivered from Satan's evil clutches.

Importunity In Prayer

In the shallow pond of today's church, I can already envision ankle-deep Christians calling prayer meetings to put these powerful principles into practice. Somewhere between their praise choruses and refreshments, they'll plan a little spiritual combat. During that fifteen minutes of their prayer group's gathering, they'll presume to prevail against the forces of darkness on behalf of the immortal souls of men. I shudder at the thought of such praying wimps attempting to do what only the bravest of prayer warriors should ever dare.

This matter of binding and loosing, of pulling down strongholds and of bringing men to obedience to Christ, should never be undertaken by the fainthearted. All who drop to their knees in this crusade for men's souls will find themselves fiercely assaulted and assailed by the adversary. Nothing provokes Apollyon more than the audacity of small bands of prayer warriors invading his territory to seize his property.

In Daniel 10:1–21, Daniel's concern for his people's destiny drove him to his knees. For three weeks, he sought God in prayer and fasting. Finally, after twenty-one days, an angel appeared with an answer to Daniel's fervent prayers. The rest of the Book of Daniel consists of an extensive revelation of the prophetic future received by the prophet in response to his prayerful importunity *(Daniel 11:1–12:13)*.

When the angel appeared, he explained how he was dispatched from Heaven on the very first day Daniel prayed. However, he was *"withstood"* for twenty-one days by *"the prince of the kingdom of Persia."* Had it not been for the intervention of *"Michael, one of the chief princes,"* the angel may never have gotten through to the prophet. After leaving Daniel, the angel had to fight his way back to Heaven for not only was *"the prince of Persia"* waiting to withstand him on his return but *"the prince of Grecia"* as well.

This rare glimpse afforded us into the spiritual realm reveals the spiritual conflict incited by the prayers of the saints. The moment Daniel dropped to his knees on behalf of his people, war broke out in the heavenlies. Demonic forces, such as *"the prince of Persia"* and *"the prince of Grecia,"* crossed swords with angelic beings, including *"Michael"* the archangel of God.

Daniel, too, was caught up in this other-worldly conflict. Indeed, it appears to be his importunity in prayer that finally won the day, yet this prayer warfare took a heavy toll on the prophet, leaving him sapped, speechless, and semiconscious. So weakened was Daniel from his warfare praying that he required supernatural strengthening no less than three times.

If we dare to drop to our knees on behalf of lost souls, especially in an attempt to pray down Satan's strongholds in their lives, we will find ourselves immediately embroiled in horrendous spiritual conflict. War will break out in the heavenlies and demonic forces will be summoned to get us off of our knees before the answer to our prayers gets through. The *"principalities," "powers," "rulers of the darkness of this world,"* and *"spiritual wickedness in high places,"* which the Apostle Paul warns us about in Ephesians 6:12, will not stand idly by while God reveals their strongholds in people's lives so that we can pray them down. Instead, they will do everything in their power to keep God's answers to our prayers from getting through.

Do you remember Jesus' explanation of why His disciples were unable to deliver the boy with an evil spirit in Mark 9: 14–29? Jesus explained, *"This kind can come forth by nothing, but by prayer and fasting."* According to Paul in Ephesians 6:12 and Jesus in Mark 9:29, there are different kinds of demons. Some are easier to deal with than others. Those who are more difficult require extended times of *"prayer and fasting"* to overcome.

Jesus' parables "The Friend at Midnight" *(Luke 11:5–8)* and "The Unjust Judge" *(Luke 18:1–6)* teach the importance of importunity in prayer. According to Luke, Jesus taught these parables so that we would learn *"to always pray, and not to faint" (Luke 18:1)*. Nowhere is our importunity in prayer more important than in our prayers for the lost. We must not give up on our intercession for lost souls, no matter how long it takes or how exhausting it becomes.

Any group of serious prayer warriors covenanting together to pull down Satan's strongholds in men's lives must be committed for the long run. There is no quick fix in the discharge of this war. It may take days, weeks, months, or even years before God's answers to our prayers break through, but the question is how long and hard are we willing to battle for the lost souls of loved ones and friends.

PRAYER

"I praise you, Lord Jesus, for destroying the works of the devil. I thank you for giving to your church the keys to the kingdom of Heaven and the power to bind and loose. As one possessing this extraordinary power, I ask you to bind the strongman and spoil his goods by stripping him of his armor and pulling down his strongholds in the lives of the lost for whom I am burdened. I also pray that the lost who are loosed by your binding of the strongman will be brought into obedience to you so that the devil will never again be given place in their lives. Amen."

Don Walton

Prayer List

- Pray that God will burden you for the lost souls He wants you to pray for.

- Pray that the gospel will be preached to the lost so that they can believe and be saved. *(1 Corinthians 1:21)*

- Pray that God will speak to your heart concerning His elect so that you can partner with God in the elect's salvation by praying for them the prayer of faith. *(James 5:15; Romans 10:17; 1 Corinthians 3:9)*

- Pray and plead the blood of Jesus Christ over the lost so that the prince of this world will be cast out of their lives. *(Luke 4:5–8; John 12:31; Revelation 5:1–10)*

- Pray that the redeemed of the Lord will say so and be saved by confessing the Lord Jesus Christ. *(1 John 2:2; 2 Peter 2:1; Psalm 107:2; Romans 10:9–10)*

- Pray that the lost will receive Jesus Christ and be given by Him the power to become the children of God. *(John 1:12)*

- Pray that the Lord of the harvest will send forth laborers into His harvest, for the harvest is great, but the laborers are few. *(Matthew 9:37–38; Luke 10:2)*

- Pray that the Lord will daily add to the church such as should be saved. *(Acts 2:47)*

- Pray that the Lord will send you or a fellow laborer to preach to the lost so that the lost will be able to hear about Christ, believe in Him, call upon His name, and be saved. *(Romans 10:13–15)*

- Pray that the Lord will daily lift up your eyes to see the fields that are white unto harvest so that you may be used by Him to gather fruit unto eternal life. *(John 4:35–38)*

- Pray for those in authority so that we will have a quiet and peaceable society in which all men will have an opportunity to come unto the knowledge of the truth and be saved. *(1 Timothy 2:14)*

- Pray for God's angels to minister to the ones who shall be heirs of salvation by sealing and safeguarding them until the day of their salvation. *(Hebrews 1:14; Revelation 73:1–8)*

- Pray for God to work His greatest miracle—THE MIRACLE OF SALVATION—on behalf of the lost. *(Mark 10:26–27)*

- Pray that God will give the gift of faith to the lost. *(Ephesians 2:8–9)*

- Pray that faith will be born in the hearts of the lost as God speaks His Word directly and personally to them through the person of the Holy Spirit. *(Romans 10:17)*

- Pray that the lost will not provoke God to anger by hardening their hearts on the day they hear His voice. *(Psalm 95:7–8; Hebrews 3:7–8,15)*

- Pray that the lost will recognize the day they hear God's voice as the day of salvation. *(2 Corinthians 6:2)*

- Pray that God will grant repentance to the lost so that they may acknowledge the truth, escape from the snare of the devil, be converted, and have their sins blotted out. *(Acts 3:19, 5:31, 11:18; 2 Timothy 2:25–26)*

- Pray that God will give the gift of tears to the lost by breaking their sinful hearts with godly sorrow, which alone produces repentance to salvation not to be repented of. *(Psalm 51:17; 2 Corinthians 7:1–11)*

- Pray that the Holy Spirit will convict the lost of sin, righteousness, and judgment. *(John 16:7–11)*

- Pray that God the Father will draw the lost to Christ. *(John 6:44, 65)*

- Pray that God's Spirit will not cease to strive with the lost. *(Genesis 6:3; Romans 1:24, 26, 28)*

- Pray that the lost will not commit the unpardonable sin by hardening their hearts and becoming calloused to the conviction of the Holy Spirit, God's final call to lost humanity. *(Matthew 12:31–32)*

- Pray that God's commandment, "Let there be light," will be spoken in the darkened and veiled hearts of the lost so that they will see the glory of God in the face of Jesus Christ. *(2 Corinthians 4:3–6; Genesis 1:1–3; Ephesians 4:18; 2 Corinthians 3:14–16)*

- Pray that the lost will receive the gospel by a revelation of Jesus Christ. *(Galatians 1:11–12)*

- Pray that God the Father will reveal to the lost that Jesus is the Christ, the Son of the living God. *(Matthew 16:13–17)*

- Pray that the lost will be enlightened and enabled by the Holy Spirit to confess: "Jesus is Lord." *(1 Corinthians 12:3)*

- Pray that Christ will be lifted up to the lost so that He can draw them unto Himself. *(John 12:32)*

- Pray that the lost will come to their senses, even if it takes the pigpen to bring them to themselves. *(Luke 15:11–24)*

- Pray that God will bind the strongman and spoil his goods by stripping him of his armor and pulling down his strongholds in the lives of the lost. *(Matthew 12:29; Mark 3:27; Luke 11:21–22; 2 Corinthians 10:3–6; Matthew 16:13–19, 18:18–20)*

NOTES

1. The fact that all men are redeemed in the limited sense of being bought back for God by the shed blood of Jesus Christ should not be confused with the fuller redemption that Scripture ascribes to believers alone. This particular redemption of the church may best be seen in Ephesians 1:14 where the Apostle Paul writes: *"Which is the earnest of our inheritance until the redemption of the purchased possession, unto the praise of his glory."* According to Paul, the Holy Spirit is God's "earnest money" deposited in our hearts as a guarantee of our inheritance. This divine guarantee of our inheritance in Christ will be made good at *"the redemption of the purchased possession."* The Greek word used for *"purchased possession"* means *"an obtaining or acquisition of a peculiar purchased possession."* Although the whole world has been bought back for God by the shed blood of Jesus Christ, the church is the *"peculiar purchased possession"* that Christ is coming again to acquire. This explains Acts 20:28 where the church is singled out from the rest of creation as being *"purchased with his* [Christ's] *own blood"* and also 1 Peter 2:9 where the saints are called God's "peculiar people" or, as the American Standard Version translates it, *"a people for God's own possession."*

    Furthermore, the church's particular redemption may be seen in the fact that she alone has been redeemed from *"the curse of the law" (Galatians 3:13)*, from the guilt of sin *(Ephesians 1:7; Colossians 1:14)*, and from *"all iniquity,"* so as to be purified and made into Christ's *"peculiar people" (Titus 2:14)* for all eternity *(Hebrews 9:12, 15)*.

2. From "It Took a Miracle" copyright 1948, renewed 1976 by John W. Peterson Music Company. All rights reserved. Used by permission.

3. Charles Spurgeon, *Morning and Evening: Daily Readings* (October 13); Public Domain.

4. From *My Utmost for His Highest* by Oswald Chambers. Copyright © 1935 by Dodd Mead and Co., renewed © 1963 by the Oswald Chambers Publications Association Ltd., and used by permission of Discovery House Publishers, Box 3566, Grand Rapids, MI 49501. All rights reserved.

5. Spurgeon, *Morning and Evening.*

6. Jonathan Edwards, "Sinners in the Hands of an Angry God," Public Domain.

7. Ibid.

8. Francis Thompson, "The Hound of Heaven," Public Domain.